METAPHYSICS WITHOUT TRUTH

METAPHYSICS WITHOUT TRUTH

ON THE IMPORTANCE OF CONSISTENCY WITHIN NIETZSCHE'S PHILOSOPHY

STEFAN LORENZ SORGNER

Marquette Studies in Philosophy

No. 50

Andrew Tallon, Series Editor

Library of Congress Cataloging-in-Publication Data

Sorgner, Stefan Lorenz.
Metaphysics without truth : on the importance of consistency within Nietzsche's philosophy / Stefan Lorenz Sorgner. — [2nd and rev. ed.].
p. cm. — (Marquette studies in philosophy ; no. 50)
Includes bibliographical references (p.) and index.
ISBN-13: 978-0-87462-673-5 (pbk. : alk. paper)
ISBN-10: 0-87462-673-0 (pbk. : alk. paper)
1. Nietzsche, Friedrich Wilhelm, 1844-1900. I. Title.
B3317.S618 2007
193—dc22

2006033787

Cover photo of the Château Vaux-le-Vicomte, France, 2003, by Andrew J. Tallon

Marquette University Press
Milwaukee

The Association of Jesuit University Presses

Contents

Foreword

TO THE REVISED SECOND EDITION

I am very happy about the responses my Nietzsche interpretation has received from various Nietzsche scholars from all over the world. Unfortunately, it was difficult for many other scholars, and university libraries to get hold of the first edition of this monograph, as it was published by a small German publishing house ("Utz Verlag" in Munich). Therefore, I am very happy that the "Marquette University Press" is willing to publish a second and revised edition of my Nietzsche interpretation. The director of "Marquette University Press," Prof. Andrew Tallon, has been extremely supportive, kind, and helpful, in getting the second edition ready for printing.

The publication of the second edition has also given me the chance to improve parts of the book: the English was polished, the formal structure of the text was altered, new secondary literature was referred to in the text, the bibliography was restructured and updated, and some arguments were put forward more detailed and others were rewritten completely. I am glad that my friend, Dr. Joe Sen from the University of London, helped me significantly in making improvements to the first edition of my Nietzsche book.

In addition, I have benefited immensely from responses, discussions, and exchanges with various scholars during recent years. I am particularly grateful to the following scholars: Prof. A. Autiero (Münster), Prof. B. Babich (Fordham), Dr. Rebecca Bamford (Emory), Prof. H. James Birx (Canisius College), Dr. I. Deretic (Belgrade), Dr. O. Fürbeth (Kassel, Frankfurt a. M.), Prof. R. Goerner (London), Prof. B. Himmelmann (Berlin), Prof. N. Knoepffler (Jena), Dr. R. Schmidt-Grépály (Weimar), Dr. D. Phillips (Oxford), Dr. M. Schramm (Leipzig), Dr. H. O. Seitschek (Munich), Dr. J. Sen (London), Prof. A. U. Sommer (Greifswald), Prof. W. Stegmaier (Greifswald), Prof. B. R. Suchla (Giessen), Prof. C. Taylor (McGill), Prof. G. Vattimo (Turin), Prof. W. Vossenkuhl (Munich), Dr. M. G. Weiß (Vienna), and Dr. H. Zude (Jena).

Finally, I wish to address a criticism, which was raised in the detailed review of Prof. A. Horn in Acta Germanica 28 (2000) (University of the Witwatersrand in South Africa). According to her, I claim the following:

> Nietzsche´s ability to contradict his own skepticism about the need to be consistent is therefore seen as an indication of Nietzsche's truth, but it could also be interpreted as proof of Nietzsche´s strength which lies in considering a problem from different points of view without fear of contradicting himself.

I wish to point out that I have never held that Nietzsche´s ability to contradict his own skepticism was as an indication of Nietzsche's truth. Firstly, I need to stress that Nietzsche did not actually contradict his own scepticism. He merely seemingly contradicted his own scepticism. Secondly, I do not regard his seemingly contradicting his own scepticism as an indication of Nietzsche's truth. It is, however, an indication of his achieving the highest feeling of power, given his own philosophy. So, Horn is correct when she puts forward that "it could also be interpreted as proof of Nietzsche´s strength," and this is also how I have interpreted Nietzsche, as he clearly holds: "To be classical, one must possess all the strong, seemingly contradictory gifts and desires—but in such a way that they go together beneath one yoke;" [WP 848]

The classical style which one can find in Nietzsche's philosophy, as it contains seemingly contradictory gifts and desires, is linked with the highest feeling of power: "The classical style is essentially a representation of this calm, simplification, abbreviation, concentration—the highest feeling of power is concentrated in the classical type." [WP 799]

Nietzsche seemingly contradicts his own scepticism, when he puts forward his metaphysics of the will to power. This is a strength, according to Nietzsche, because it is a quality which is connected to the classical style. Whatever is classical possesses "seemingly contradictory gifts and desires," according to Nietzsche, and "the highest feeling of power is concentrated in the classical type." As Nietzsche's philosophy contains "seemingly contradictory gifts and desires," Nietzsche as the creator of his philosophy has reached the "highest feeling of power." The world and all things in it are nothing but will to power. Therefore, Nietzsche also is will to power, and it is his goal to achieve the highest feeling of power. By putting forward a classically styled philosophy, he manages to reach his goal, as "the highest feeling of power is concentrated in the classical type," and Nietzsche as the originator of his philosophy is part of his philosophy, and so Nietzsche together with his philosophy manages to reach the highest feeling of power which is also his main goal.

I am very much looking forward to the responses and reactions to the second and revised edition of my Nietzsche interpretation.

Acknowledgements

I am very grateful for Dr. Paddy Fitzpatrick's excellent translations of certain aphorisms of Nietzsche. Many thanks to Dr. Paul MacDonald for the laborious task of proofreading the work. My supervisor at the University of Durham, Chris Long, was a model of academic support; to him I owe my greatest intellectual debts for this book.

In addition, I want to mention my friend and former tutor at King's College, University of London, Dr. Joe Sen. This study is deeply indebted to him as a result of our many rewarding discussions about Nietzsche. He has also proofread the revised version of this book. Another philosopher from King's who influenced my way of thinking enormously is Prof. Dr. M. M. McCabe. She forced me to express myself clearly, rigorously and carefully and I am extremely thankful for these lessons. Incredibly important for my philosophical career in general are Prof. Dr. David Cooper (Durham/UK), Prof. Dr. Niko Knoepffler (Jena/Germany), Prof. H. James Birx Buffalo/USA), Prof. Dr. Beate Regina Suchla (Goettingen/Germany), and Prof. Dr. Gianni Vattimo (Turin/Italy). All of them have supported my philosophical endeavours for a very long time.

I am extremely grateful to my grandparents, Theresia and Albert Guha and Anna and Georg Sorgner, who have been caring, reliable, and loving. Most thanks go to my parents, Karin and Lorenz Sorgner, who have always provided me with all the love and support I needed.

Note

ON TEXTS AND ABBREVIATIONS

In order to minimize footnotes and to eliminate the inconvenience of endnotes I have incorporated almost all references to secondary sources into the text, citing only the author's name (unless it is clear from the context) and the publication date. If necessary, I also mention the page (P.) or chapter (chap.) number. The works cited are listed in the Bibliography.

For Nietzsche's work I have used the "*Kritische Studienausgabe*" (KSA) edited by Giorgio Colli and Mazzino Montinari (Munich: Deutscher Taschenbuch Verlag GmbH & Co. KG, 1967-1977). I generally follow the excellent translations into English listed below. I am grateful to Dr. Paddy Fitzpatrick from University of Durham for the translation of certain aphorisms, these translations are signified by the 'PF' after the reference.

As it is still common in the English speaking world to refer to "The Will to Power," I will do so, too. For those, who wish to find the corresponding German original, Scott Simmon's "Concordance: Will to Power * KGW/KSA" (In: The New Nietzsche Studies. Vol. 1:½, Fall/Winter 1996, P. 126-153) is particularly helpful.

I cite Nietzsche's works by the Initials of their English titles and the section number. I list here the abbreviations in the text and the works to which they refer.

BT = *Die Geburt der Tragödie*
Nietzsche, Friedrich "The Birth of Tragedy; The Case of Wagner" translated from the German by Walter Kaufmann (New York: Random House, Inc., 1967)

UM = *Unzeitgemässe Betrachtungen*
Nietzsche, Friedrich "Untimely Meditations" translated from the German by R. J. Hollingdale (Cambridge: Cambridge Univerrsity Press, 1983)

HAH = *Menschliches Allzumenschliches*
Nietzsche, Friedrich "Human, All too Human" translated from the German by R. J. Hollingdale (Cambridge: Cambridge University Press, 1996)

D = *Morgenröte*
Nietzsche, Friedrich "Daybreak" translated from the German by R. J. Hollingdale (Cambridge: Cambridge University Press, 1982)

GS = *Die fröhliche Wissenschaft*
Nietzsche, Friedrich "The Gay Science" translated from the German by Walter Kaufmann (New York: Random House, Inc., 1974)

Z = *Also sprach Zarathustra*
Nietzsche, Friedrich "The Portable Nietzsche" selectet and translated from the German by Walter Kaufmann (New York: The Viking Press, Inc., 1954)

BGE = *Jenseits von Gut und Böse*
GM = *Die Genealogie der Moral*
Nietzsche, Friedrich "On the Genealogy of Morals; Ecce Homo" translated from the German by Walter Kaufmann (New York: Random House, Inc., 1967)
Nietzsche, Friedrich "Beyond Good and Evil" translated from the German by R. J. Hollingdale (London: Penguin Books Ltd., 1973)

NW = *Nietzsche contra Wagner*
Nietzsche, Friedrich "The Portable Nietzsche" selectet and translated from the German by Walter Kaufmann (New York: The Viking Press, Inc., 1954)

WP = *Der Wille zur Macht*
Nietzsche, Friedrich "Der Wille zur Macht" Nachwort: A. Baeumler (Stuttgart: Alfred Kröner Verlag, 1964)
Nietzsche, Friedrich "The Will to Power" translated from the German by Walter Kaufmann and R. J. Hollingdale (London: Weidenfeld and Nicholson, 1968)

TI = *Götzendämmerung*
AC = *Der Antichrist*
EH = *Ecce Homo*
Nietzsche, Friedrich "On the Genealogy of Morals; Ecce Homo" translated from the German by Walter Kaufmann (New York: Random House, Inc., 1967)
Nietzsche, Friedrich "The Portable Nietzsche" selectet and translated from the German by Walter Kaufmann (New York: The Viking Press, Inc., 1954)

PTG = *Die Philosophie im tragischen Zeitalter der Griechen*
HC = *Homers Wettkampf*
TLN = *Ueber Wahrheit und Lüge im aussermoralischen Sinne*
UP = *Wir Philologen*
Nietzsche, Friedrich: "Kritische Studienausgabe (KSA)" edited by Giorgio Colli and Mazzino Montinari (Munich: Deutscher Taschenbuch Verlag GmbH & Co. KG, 1967-1977).

Introduction

1

1.1 The Problem & my Solution (in brief)

The problem which I will solve within this book is how Nietzsche can consistently put forward a metaphysics while also holding that whatever he says is not true. The problem is an important one because with his denial of the truth Nietzsche had a significant influence on philosophy in the twentieth century—he became the inspiration of post-modernism whose proponents deny the possibility that human beings ever get to know the truth. All post-modernist philosophers have to have a reply to the liar paradox, and they also have to explain why what they have to say matters, because if they themselves claim that what they say is not true, it is not obvious why one should listen to what they have to say. Nehamas showed convincingly that in Nietzsche's case the liar paradox does not apply, for within his philosophy 'no one is obliged to believe' [Nehamas (1985): P. 67] what Nietzsche said [Nehamas (1985): chap. 2]. However, Nehamas, as well as all the other interpreters, does not have a suitable reply to the second question. All he says is that Nietzsche's philosophy implies that 'one's own views are the best for oneself without implying that they need be good for anyone else' [Nehamas (1985): P.72] which is not a satisfying reply because it does not explain why anyone should listen to what Nietzsche has to say. I will be more explicit about this in the last main part where I also present my complete reply to this question; this will lead to the conclusion that Nietzsche regards his philosophy as superior because he expects it to appeal to the spirit of future times.

As the problem which I will solve with this book already suggests, the book is principally exegetical. I will not discuss whether Nietzsche's philosophy is plausible or not, and I also will not point out where Nietzsche, according to my mind, has gone wrong. All I will do is to put forward a new interpretation of the areas of Nietzsche's philosophy[1] relevant to the problem in question, and I will apply Augustine's principle of charity: "what is read must be diligently turned over in the

1 An outstanding general introduction to Nietzsche's philosophy was given by Vattimo [Vattimo (1992)].

mind until an interpretation is found that promotes the reign of charity" [quoted in Beardsley (1966): P. 109], for I think that this is what a good interpreter has to do.

Before I can begin with any further details of my book, I have to clarify the use of some ambiguous or unclear notions. Although I try to give a clear definition whenever it is necessary within the text, I wish to state some definitions at the outset, e.g. the meanings of the notions of the title of the book.

1.2 Some Definitions

Metaphysics: Metaphysics can have (at least) two different meanings. It can mean either philosophy of two world theories, or philosophy of the nature of the world. In the first case, metaphysics refers to such philosophies as put forward by Plato or Kant. In the second case, it simply refers to any ultimate description of the world. Nietzsche is a critic of metaphysics, if the notion is used in the first sense; but he is putting forward one of his own, if we take the second sense of the notion. The expression "metaphysics" in the title of this book has to be read using the second of the above mentioned senses.

Truth: Truth can refer to many different theories; the pragmatic, coherence, and correspondence theories of truth are the most common ones. Within the book, I will always clarify which theory of truth I am referring to. In the title of the book, I am referring to (a version of) the correspondence theory of truth.

Ontology: Ontology is another expression for and can be taken as equivalent to the second sense of the notion "metaphysics" (philosophy of the ultimate nature of the world), for it means the teaching/word (*logos*) of Being (*ens*). Nietzsche puts forward a number of distinctive claims which comprise an ontology.

Apollo: The first main part is entitled 'Apollo' and this means the creative force. It includes the creative force in human beings, as well as that in the rest of the world. However, I will mostly be concerned with it with respect to human beings. Still, I do not define it in such a restrictive way, because it is essential that it applies to all kinds of creative forces.

Dionysos: The second main part is entitled 'Dionysos' and this refers to the destructive force. It includes the destructive force in human beings, as well as in the rest of the world. However, I will mostly be concerned with it with respect to human beings. Still, I do not define it in such a restrictive way, because it is essential that it applies to all kinds of destructive forces.

Platonism: Platonism always implies the concept of a two world theory. The expression 'two world theory' means a theory which puts forward that two separate worlds exist.

2

2.1 On Nietzsche's unpublished Work

It has been a much discussed topic which attitude one should take with respect to Nietzsche's unpublished work, and due to the vast amount and possible significance of this work every interpreter has to take a clear position in that respect. One can distinguish three main camps which the principal Nietzsche interpreters fall into. Firstly, there are the interpreters like Maudemarie Clark who rely almost exclusively on Nietzsche's published work. Secondly, there are the ones who agree with Derrida's position which accords an equality of value between the published, and unpublished work. Thirdly, there are the followers of Heidegger who regard the unpublished work to be of superior value in comparison to the published work.

According to Clark,"it seems a good idea to hold off on the use of the Nachlass as long as possible since the published writings provide much more of a context for specific passages and therefore many more checks on the accuracy of interpretation." [Clark (1990): P. 26]. This, however, is not an argument which explains why we should regard Nietzsche's published work as containing his mature philosophy. The most it establishes is that his published writings provide interpreters with a more accurate basis for interpretation, than do his unpublished writings. I am not denying this, but this position only implies that one has to be particularly careful when dealing with his unpublished writings.

Another argument Clark put forward was that Nietzsche's unpublished notes contain a philosophy which "is usually philosophically weaker" [Clark (1990): P. 26] than the one in his published work, which she tries to establish with her interpretation. I think that one should read the competing interpretations of Nietzsche, take into consideration how many rather unambiguous statements Clark has to explain in a rather strange manner, and how the very same statements can also be interpreted (best example: Nietzsche's denial of the truth), and then one should judge for oneself which position is the more plausible. I am certain that it becomes clear that Nietzsche's unpublished notes can and often do contain arguments and positions which are philosophically stronger and more interesting than the ones from his published writings.

The most interesting and informed discussion of Nietzsche's unpublished work which defends the superiority of Nietzsche's published work can be found in Bernd Magnus' essay "The Use and Abuse of the Will to Power" [ed. Solomon (1988): P. 218—235]. He points out that by the end of 1888 Nietzsche no longer wished to publish a work called "The Will to Power" and that the available text is based upon one of Nietzsche's plans for his main work—but not even a very special plan. All this is correct as I have argued before. I agree with Magnus that the notes contained in the current text of "The Will to Power" are in no way superior to his other unpublished notes. This is, however, all Magnus can establish with his previously mentioned position. Magnus also claims that "'Der Antichrist' displaces the 'Umwerthung' as the title of that 'major' planned work" [ed. Solomon (1988): P. 230]. This is also correct. However, it does not imply that interpreters should not refer to his unpublished notes.

I do have some sympathy for Heidegger's position, as his unpublished writings seem to me as philosophically more interesting than his published writings, but wish to stress that I share Nehamas general approach concerning Nietzsche's writings: He claims: "Nietzsche is an author, a public figure, and all his writings are relevant to his interpretation. The importance we attach to any part of his work cannot depend on general principles about which is essentially primary and which necessarily follows. The importance of each text depends on the specific contribution that text makes to our construction of a coherent and understandable whole. It must be determined separately in each individual case." [Nehamas (1985), P. 10].

Therefore, I will refer both to Nietzsche's published as well as his unpublished writings. In particular, I will focus upon his writings from the third, and last period which, according to my mind, begins with the publication of "The Gay Science" in 1882. In that period, Nietzsche's thinking is mature, philosophically interesting, and relevant also for our current philosophical problems.

3

3.1 On some other Interpretations of Nietzsche's Philosophy

I will mention other interpreters of Nietzsche's work within my own interpretation, whenever I regard the reference as clarification of my own position. However, most of the traditional great interpretations of Nietzsche are so different from my own that here at the outset I will only point out the essential differences and problems they have to face. I will always focus my main attention on the overall categories of truth and metaphysics. Each interpreter stresses different categories in Nietzsche, however these two are usually dealt with, whereas such special sub-categories as nihilism, to which I attribute a lot of weight, are often left out in many interpretations.

The first, and arguably, greatest interpreter of Niezsche with whom I will briefly be concerned is Heidegger [1961]. He claims that Nietzsche's theory of the will to power (= WP) and his theory of the eternal recurrence of everything (= ER) are metaphysical theories which make a claim to correspond to the truth. However, he also holds that Nietzsche was a critic of metaphysics; so on Heidegger's account Nietzsche's philosophy is inconsistent. According to him, Nietzsche aims to overcome nihilism by overcoming metaphysics, but does not manage this. It is correct that Nietzsche tries to overcome nihilism and it is also correct that he was a critic of metaphysics in one sense of the word, though not the sense in which I am using it. Nietzsche is only a critic of metaphysics in the sense that he attacks two world theories, as they are popular in the Platonic-Christian tradition. Yet, he tries to overcome nihilism by putting forward a new metaphysics in the second sense of the word [main part 3 of this book]. Heidegger failed to realise that whenever Nietzsche criticised metaphysics he was using the term to mean philosophy of two world theories but that the metaphysics Nietzsche put forward was a one world theory and that metaphysics in this case has to be taken to mean the philosophy of the ultimate nature of the world. In this case, it does not follow, as it does in Heidegger's interpretation, that Nietzsche's philosophy is inconsistent. One reason in favour of my interpretation is the fact that Nietzsche values consistency extremely highly [WP 515]. Although Nietzsche holds that our intellect cannot provide us with "the truth," he claims that our intellect is essential for our survival, and that his philosophy is life enhancing [WP 1052]. Therefore his philosophy has to appeal to the intellect, i.e. it has to be consistent. According to Heidegger's interpretation Nietzsche's philosophy is inconsistent. This is one main reason which goes against Heidegger's interpretation.

The next interpreter I wish to mention is Danto [1965]. According to him, Nietzsche denies the correspondence but affirms the pragmatic theory of truth. Yet, Danto also realises that WP and ER are metaphysical theories, which are supposedly making a claim to correspond to the truth. This, however, is something he cannot reconcile with the former claim. I regard Danto's to be one of the best interpretations so far, because the WP and ER are metaphysical theories, and what Nietzsche puts forward can be seen as a pragmatic theory of truth, although I would be reluctant to put it like this. Yet, Danto fails to link these positions, because his understanding of what the WP implies has been too limited. Nietzsche refers to the WP and ER as "Nietzsche's truth," which is a sub-group of "*truths*," which are all false with respect to "the truth" (in the absolute sense)[2]. Yet, this is what is essential, because "the truth" is not life affirming, and cannot be had by anyone or anything. In this way, Nietzsche does reject the correspondence theory of truth. Yet, I would be hesitant to attribute to Nietzsche the pragmatic theory of truth, because what he puts forward is false with respect to "the truth." On the other hand, Nietzsche himself refers to his theories as "Nietzsche's truth," so one could be justified in seeing it as an illustration of the pragmatic theory of truth. At this stage one has to ask what the pragmatic theory of truth implies. According to Danto it implies "whether it works in life" [Danto (1965): P. 230], but he is not certain himself whether this is an appropriate criterion or not, because he is unclear about this point himself [Danto (1965): P. 230]. What does this "whether it works in life" mean and whose life does it refer to? Given Nietzsche's perspectivism, it can only refer to Nietzsche's own life, but then the question arises why anyone else should believe in it. This clearly poses a problem for Danto's account which I will be able to solve by showing that Nietzsche thinks that his philosophy will be regarded as superior, because it appeals to the spirit of our times. Müller-Lauter and Grimm have a deeper understanding of what the pragmatic theory of truth implies. According to them, Nietzsche holds the pragmatic theory of truth, which means that for him what is pragmatic is true, what increases the feeling of power is pragmatic and Nietzsche's philosophy increases his feeling of power. This is correct, as

2 I clarify the several meanings of 'truth' later in the book.

I will show. However, both of them fail to explain why the WP and ER do let the feeling of power increase in Nietzsche, and why Nietzsche puts forward his theories, if they mainly increase his feeling of power. This I will set out in detail within my book.

A completely different Nietzsche can be found in France. There he was cultivated heavily by all sorts of thinkers and philosophers who have used him rather idiosyncratically. According to Derrida metaphysical assumptions are built within our grammar, so we cannot utter a proposition without affirming a metaphysical statement (metaphysics meaning philosophies of two world theories). Nietzsche, by rejecting metaphysics, is bound to be caught in metaphysics by default. This, however, Nietzsche has pointed out himself [TI "'Reason' in Philosophy" 5], yet he is not putting it as strongly as Derrida does, but merely hints at the possibility of this being so. I think that Nietzsche's position is superior to Derrida's, because Derrida's statement seems to me to be simply false. If Derrida was correct, then it would be impossible to put forward a monistic and a dualistic philosophy within the same language. However, Kant held a dualistic metaphysics, and Nietzsche a monistic one, but both wrote in German. This should count as a reason against Derrida's statement in question.

After these brief summaries and discussions of some of the better known interpretations of Nietzsche, I wish to stress a couple of arguments which I regard as particularly helpful. Jasper's statement that something has to be true for it to be regarded as true [Jaspers (1947): P. 198], or Nehamas claim about perspectivism that it concedes that no one is obliged to believe its thesis which implies that it is not self-refuting [Nehamas (1985): P. 67] are particularly noteworthy. The topic on which I disagree with most interpreters is the ER. Usually this theory is interpreted as an ethical test, and whenever it was taken in an metaphysical manner, it is generally regarded to be Nietzsche's greatest failure, an unbearable view with respect to modern science, and too absurd to be considered seriously. However, I take Nietzsche seriously in that respect. He regarded ER to be his deepest insight, and I will show that ER as a metaphysical theory has to be taken seriously. Of course, I am not excluding the ethical aspect from my considerations, but I regard the metaphysical to be the level on which the theory is of primary importance.

4

4.1 Philosophers as the Defenders of their own Prejudices

In this section I will introduce my understanding of Nietzsche's philosophy by dealing with two different topics. Firstly, I will try to set out and explain what Nietzsche meant when he made the statement that philosophers are just defenders of their own prejudices as he does in the following aphorism, for in this way one can get access to Nietzsche's manner of thinking:

> ...while what happens at bottom is that a prejudice, a notion, an 'inspiration', generally a desire of the heart sifted and made abstract, is defended by them with reasons sought after the event—they are one and all advocates who do not want to be regarded as such, and for the most part no better than cunning pleaders for their prejudices, which they baptize 'truths'.. [BGE 1, 5]

While interpreting the above mentioned aphorism I will criticise some claims philosophers traditionally made and try to lay open what philosophers at most can do. Secondly, I will deal with Nietzsche's approach to philosophy which does not have to face the criticism I made with respect to other philosophers.

I will set out the implications of the above mentioned claim that philosophers are just the defenders of their prejudices by dealing with the question of what the sole ultimate starting point of philosophy is.

In the history of philosophy one broadly finds two different approaches to philosophy. Most philosophers, especially since Descartes, regarded epistemology to be at the heart of philosophy, i.e. the sole ultimate starting point of philosophy. In very recent times a second approach was rediscovered by Heidegger who regards metaphysics as the centre of philosophy, an approach which can also be found in many Pre-Socratic philosophers.

I wish to mention the following problem these two approaches have to face. However, I do not have the space to prove what I am putting forward. I am claiming that neither epistemology nor metaphysics can be used as a sole ultimate starting point, so that it is deceptive to speak of either of them as the sole ultimate starting point to philosophy from which everything else is derived. I will defend the thesis that no discipline of philosophy is prior to the other. After I have given some examples which support this thesis I will put forward a further hypothesis, which had its origin in Schopenhauer in "The Fourfold Root of the Principle of Sufficient Reason" [Schopenhauer (1977)]. This further hypothesis contends that all philosophers not only cannot have started from one ultimate starting point, but that every great philosopher had to have some special, (fairly) coherent insights in the different disciplines of philosophy (e.g. metaphysics, epistemology, ethics, and aesthetics) and all they did was to present them in long lines of argument, as if one was necessitated by the other although actually the basis of their whole philosophy consisted of a few (or many) (fairly) consistent insights in the separate, but inter-related disciplines, which I have just mentioned. The separateness of epistemology and metaphysics, on the one hand, and ethical and aesthetical values, on the other, will be supported by Hume's argument that one cannot derive an 'ought' from an 'is' and I will try to make the separateness, but interrelatedness of the disciplines of metaphysics and epistemology obvious in the following. After that I will combine the claims that there is no sole ultimate starting point to philosophy and that all philosophies are based on insights and this will lead me to the conclusion that the insights out of which all philosophies are constructed are not insights into the truth but prejudices of the individual philosophers.

If the following points seem plausible and the problems mentioned serious enough, then Nietzsche's approach to philosophy offers an appropriate alternative understanding of philosophy which goes round many of the problems traditional philosophies have to face. Of course, this new approach creates new problems. The main parts of this book will then try to state some replies to the new problems.

What is the appropriate starting point to philosophy? In the history of philosophy one main party has claimed it is epistemology, another that it is metaphysics. First, I will explain why it cannot be epistemology, then why it cannot be metaphysics and in the end I will describe the starting point which philosophers are left with; namely the personal prejudices of the philosophers with respect to the different disciplines of philosophy (e.g. metaphysics, epistemology, ethics).

The first problem epistemology has to face is an argument by Hegel which goes against the possibility of epistemology—Nietzsche's philosophy provides an answer to this problem as well. It can be stated as follows:

Whenever one starts an epistemological enquiry, one is looking for a way to gain knowledge of the world. Yet, to be able to realise that one has actually found what one is looking for (a way to gain knowledge of the world) one needs a criterion on the basis of which we can decide whether we have found it or not. However, this criterion is actually what we are looking for. Therefore we cannot even get started.

This argument goes against the possibility of epistemology. I will mention an appropriate reply to it later; what I am claiming now is something further. If one accepts the possibility of epistemology, then one also needs to have a metaphysical system which does not come after epistemology. Let me state one example: empiricists hold that all our knowledge comes from our sense perceptions. Prior to any sense perception our mind is empty; it does not contain any innate ideas. There cannot be anything within our minds which has not been perceived by the senses before. Our mind is a blank tablet (*tabula rasa*) prior to any sense impression. John Locke was one of the first philosophers to formulate this clearly.

The problem with this position is how this can be the basis of a philosophy. It clearly presupposes the notion "mind" and therefore must also presuppose a picture of the mind and with this some sort of metaphysics. Locke regarded the mind to be an immaterial thing, whereas the objects it perceives are physical things. So epistemology cannot be the sole ultimate starting point to this philosophy because to be able to deal with epistemology it needs a metaphysics declaring that there are immaterial and material objects (If Locke had regarded the mind to be a material thing, then my argument would have applied as well, only with a different metaphysics as a basis). The metaphysics does not come after the epistemology, so epistemology cannot be the sole starting point. This, according to my mind, applies to all other epistemologically based philosophies as well.

Secondly, there are philosophers who regard metaphysics as the sole ultimate starting point to philosophy, e.g. the Pre-Socratics, Heidegger.

The method of starting philosophical enquiry with metaphysics was brought back into our consciousness by Heidegger. "He demands, first, a reversal of the 'modern' priority of epistemology over ontology—of enquiries into knowledge over ones into existence. Knowledge 'in the usual spectator sense ... presupposes existence' (BP 276), since no account of knowledge is possible without a prior understanding of the nature of knowers and what they know. The crucial issue is begged when it is assumed that we are simply 'thinking things' confronted by extended ones, the only problem then being how we escape from our 'inner spheres' so as to acquire knowledge about these external objects. A second, related reversal Heidegger demands is the move from 'the considerations of beings [entities] to the ... thematization of Being' (BP 227)." [Cooper (1996): P. 21].

Yet, Heidegger only brought this approach towards philosophy back into the forefront of our philosophical concerns. In the Pre-Socratic era philosophers such as Thales, Anaximander, Anaximenes had already regarded metaphysics as the basis of philosophy. Especially these Milesian natural philosophers provide us with prime examples for this sort of approach to philosophy. Thales for example regarded water to be the one original substance out of which everything else developed. For Anaximander Being was something indefinite and unlimited (Greek: *apeiron*). Anaximenes held that air is the original substance. Yet, what all of them had in common was that they tried to explain the creation of all "Seienden" (beings, entities) by reference to an ultimate original substance.

In all of these cases metaphysics is regarded as the basis of philosophy. Still, it seems to me that this could not be the sole ultimate basis of a philosophy. Of course, someone could hold that the world is a physical devil. Yet, no one would regard this person to be a philosopher, merely by asserting this. A philosopher needs justified epistemic reasons for holding this view as in the case of Parmenides who claims that there is only Being and no Becoming. To defend this metaphysics which was Parmenides' ultimate starting point in philosophy, Zeno of Elea (Parmenides' pupil) put forward arguments which showed that every other view leads to a contradiction, e.g. an "arrow cannot move because it is always in a place equal to itself and if it is in a place equal to itself, then it is at rest—so it is always at rest." This, supposedly, implies that every other metaphysical view is untenable or incorrect; an allegedly syllogistic argument is used by Zeno to support the metaphysics of Parmenides. Again, it is not the metaphysics which serves as the sole ultimate foundation and brings about the epistemology, because it is assumed that what is contradictory cannot correspond to reality. This is the epistemological assumption without which Parmenides could not have built his metaphysics. Therefore epistemology in this case as well cannot have come after the metaphysics, because it provides us with the reasons to hold his metaphysical view.

So far, I have stated some reasons in favour of the position that neither metaphysics nor epistemology can serve us as the sole ultimate starting point to philosophy. It seems necessary that one discipline demands the other. Concerning the relationship of epistemology and metaphysics, there are two possibilities: it could either be the case that one is prior to the other, but then the other would have to be prior to the first as well (This would render any approach ad absurdum, as I have just tried to show), or neither is prior to the other but both belong to the same level and are separate, though inter-related, i.e. not completely separate[3]. The latter option seems to me to be the only defensible one.

This leads me to the next point that philosophy is not mainly about arguing, but about insights (prejudices) in the different branches of philosophy (epistemology, metaphysics et cetera). This must now be clarified.

Firstly, I would briefly like to reconsider what a deductive argument consists of. An argument consists of the premises, the method of inference and the conclusion. Where do the premises come from? One option would be that they stem from another argument. Yet, how can one justify the initial premises and the initial method of inference? One can only refer to their internal plausibility and their consistency with respect to the other premises we hold. There cannot be any further justification as it seems to me. These premises provide one with the basis of ones philosophy. From these each philosophy derives all the details of its content. So a great philosopher seems to be one who had many innovative, consistent insights. His arguments do not seem to be as important for philosophy as they are taken to be because in an argument one can only derive something as a conclusion which was already contained in the premises. So the conclusions of arguments cannot provide us with any new insight which has not been in the premises before. An argument can only show whether a system is internally consistent and which view a philosopher could or would take with respect to a certain question but the basis of each philosophy can only be a set of insights with the aforementioned characteristics. How else should he get the initial method of inference and the initial premises? Let us

3 They have to be separate, because metaphysics describes the ultimate reality, but epistemology tells us how we get to know it. These are clearly separate categories. Still, they must be inter-related, because the content of these two categories must not be inconsistent. Consistency is the basis for the evaluation of a philosophy.

apply this point to Hegel's critique of epistemology. If it is correct, as it seems that in arguments a philosopher cannot gain any knowledge which was not implicit in the initial premises and method of inference, then epistemology cannot be about trying to find the correct theory of knowledge through arguing, because the one which one ends up with clearly has to have been contained in the premises.

Of course, philosophers need to be able to make inferences (i.e. need to argue) to think through their system so that it contains as few inconsistencies as possible (or even none in the ideal case). Another reason why philosophers use arguments to present their views is that one can in this way represent the system, its consequences and its inner relations, so that its plausibility becomes obvious. However, one should always bear in mind that arguments cannot provide us with new knowledge. The conclusion always is already contained in the premises. We cannot derive anything new via an argument. It can only lay bare the consequences which are already contained in the premises and the method of inference.

Now we have to remember what I have tried to make plausible before, namely that neither metaphysics nor epistemology can serve us as a sole, ultimate basis for philosophy. In this way, I have come to the conclusion that it is most plausible that both of them belong to the same basic level and are separated, but inter-related. We can now apply our recently gained understanding about the importance of insights in philosophy to this. Doing so, we have to declare that a great philosopher has to have many, innovative, consistent insights with respect to the two separate, but inter-related categories of metaphysics and epistemology (and probably also logic and methodology, so that he is in a position to make further inferences from his initial insights).

Still, this obviously does not yet provide us with the basis to answer all questions of philosophy, because the disciplines of ethics, aesthetics and political philosophy, i.e. the branches which deal with value questions, are not dealt with yet. That we cannot derive these disciplines from the former was explained fairly convincingly by David Hume "A Treatise of Human Nature" (3, I, 1). There it was shown why we cannot derive an "ought" from an "is" (values from facts). So a philosopher who also deals with value questions has to have had some more insights with respect to these branches. This would lead us to the position that every great philosopher has had, as a basis, a number of insights with respect to the different disciplines he was dealing with, which traditionally were epistemology, metaphysics, ethics, aesthetics and political philosophy. These categories and their insights were separate, but inter-related.

This analysis does not yet refute the traditional philosophies. It only attacks their claim that either epistemology or metaphysics are at the heart of philosophy. Traditional rationalist philosophies could accept my analysis and say that the insights are not personal but they are related to a realm of absolute knowledge. I cannot exclude this possibility but if one takes into consideration how many philosophies there are, and how much they differ from one another, then this provides us with a genuine reason to reject this possibility.

If I wanted to sound polemical, I would say that all the different "*truths*" philosophers have put forward are nothing but certain personal prejudices (insights) and the arguments were just a means to make these plausible (among other things). Of course, defenders of this system have to face new problems, problems which I will deal with later.

This summary will, I hope, be fairly useful, for an appreciation of Nietzsche's philosophy, for I think this is what Nietzsche meant when he explained that what philosophers do is the following:

> ...while what happens at bottom is that a prejudice, a notion, an 'inspiration', generally a desire of the heart sifted and made abstract, is defended by them with reasons sought after the event—they are one and all advocates who do not want to be regarded as such, and for the most part no better than cunning pleaders for their prejudices, which they babtize 'truths'... [BGE 1, 5]

Since Nietzsche applies the same principles which he uses for other philosophies to his own philosophy as well, Nietzsche cannot and does not claim that he is putting forward "the truth." How he can consistently do this should have become clear by the end of my book.

4.2. Nietzsche's Approach to Philosophy

To be able to understand what Nietzsche was after we first have to give an insight into Nietzsche's own way to philosophy. Why did he start to philosophise? What does his way to philosophy imply for his definition of philosophy?

Originally, "philosopher" means lover (*philos*) of wisdom (*sophia*). However, many modern philosophers (e.g. from the Vienna Circle) seem to have presupposed that "philosopher" has to be understood as lover (*philos*) of the truth (*aletheia*), although this is clearly the wrong way to translate it. The correct translation of philosophy as love of wisdom is one modern philosophy seems to have forgotten. I will now also be concerned with the question which implications these two manners of understanding the notion "philosophy" have on the way philosophy is pursued, and what the aims of the philosophers are. By the way the pre 600 B. C. Greeks who have thought about the world, life, truth and wisdom had not called themselves "*philosophos*," but "*sophos*," which means "wise man." Pythagoras was the first to practise some sort of humility and introduced the term "*philosophos*," which means "lover of wisdom." I will show that for Nietzsche philosophy was the love of wisdom, and wisdom was related to value statements.

To be able to grasp Nietzsche's understanding of philosophy, we have to have a little bit of knowledge about his background and his development towards being a philosopher. He was born into a traditionally Lutheran family on the 15th of October 1844 in Röcken. His father and both of his grandfathers were Lutheran clergyman. His father died at the age of 36 when Nietzsche was only four years old. From then on all the other members of the household, in which he was living, were female. There was his mother, his (in)famous sister, and two aunts (two unmarried sisters of his father). All of them were strict believers and so the values and the world view, on which he was brought up, were Lutheran. Lutheranism is the original form of Protestant Christianity. The Lutheran understanding of the world is diametrically opposed to the ones he became familiar with at Pforta, the all-boys boarding school which Nietzsche attended and which produced many leading German intellectuals (Novalis, Fichte, Klopstock, Ranke, the brothers Schlegel). At Pforta he received a brilliant classical education. Classics, religion and German literature were the subjects he did exceptionally well in. The classics, however, which were strongly represented in this school, presented a completely different picture of the world and values from the one he used to believe in. In this way Nietzsche realised the arbitrariness of the present Christian metaphysics and value system, which was the philosophy or rather theology that he was brought up on[4]. During the years at Pforta he gradually abandoned Christianity;

4 Although, he had the possibility of deciding that Christianity is the highest form of a belief system—the closest we can come to the truth, yet. However, as he drew the inference that it is just one out of many, one can see that he does not think that the world has a determined form.

the content of what was taught at Pforta was especially influential, because it took place during his teenage years which is usually the time in which one is looking for one's own values in which one tries to free oneself from the constraints of one's family to become an individual. This is the time when one abandons ones "Ueber-Ich" and creates an "Ich Ideal" which one then tries to achieve in the future. It is not so much that Nietzsche replaced the Christian system with the Ancient Greek one but rather that the realisation of the arbitrariness of these systems made him abandon Christianity. This process is best represented in the "Genealogy of Morals" in which exactly this process is demonstrated. By the time he left Pforta the process of the abandonment of Christianity was more or less completed.

The process was probably supported by the fact that the history of his illnesses already begun when he attended Pforta (he was short-sighted and often plagued by migraine headache [Kaufmann (1974): P. 23]). The Lutheran church teaches that whatever happens corresponds to the will of God. It is of course hard to love a God who is the reason for one's own suffering; even harder if one realises that the God does not necessarily exist. Yet, this is of course only one factor which brought about Nietzsche's rejection of Christianity.

The insight that the values and the metaphysics he was brought up with are not necessary, made him face the problem of his own belief system. It created in him the will to find a new system—one that he could relate to—, because if one *believes* in some metaphysical and value system then one always knows how to act. It provides a basis, upon which one can decide what is the right choice for oneself, and a sense of stability which all of us need to survive. Nietzsche was aware of this: "...the unhistorical and the historical are necessary in equal measure for the health of an individual, of a people, and of a culture." [UM 2, 1]

The historical refers to the awareness of the great variety of systems which have been most powerful (in the section 'Dionysos'), and the unhistorical refers to some stable system or perhaps better interpretation of the world, which one needs oneself (in the section 'Apollo'). While Nietzsche was at university he discovered Schopenhauer, but his system also did not correspond to his demands, so in the end he had to transcend it as well. Yet, I do not now wish to concern myself with his personal development, but with the question I had asked before: What made him turn to philosophy? The answer to this is the loss of his old Lutheran faith by realising the contingency of metaphysical and value systems. The belief system and the values he used to live by he considered were no longer universally valid. This made him wonder whether there were no other systems or values which were better (in whatever respect) for himself. Primarily, it was not the metaphysics but the value system he needed because this one needs at every moment. Whenever one makes a decision, by choosing one thing rather than another, one evaluates this thing higher than the other thing. So what he was in need of was a new value system: "All the sciences have from now on to prepare the way for the future task of the philosophers: this task understood as the solution of the problem of value, the determination of the order of rank of values." [GM 1. Essay note]

Although the theory of value was Nietzsche's main concern he also had to deal with metaphysical questions because value systems always find their ultimate justification in a metaphysics. Nietzsche who has traditionally been referred to as the major critic of metaphysics acknowledges this himself:

> In regard to philosophical metaphysics, I see more and more who are making for the negative goal (that all positive metaphysics is an error) but still few who are taking a few steps back; for one may well look out over the topmost rung of the ladder, but one ought not to want to stand on it. The most enlightened get only as far as liberating themselves from metaphysics and looking back on it from above; whereas here too, as in the hippodrome, at the end of the track it is necessary to turn the corner. [HAH 1, 20]

What he means when he says that one has to go beyond the state in which one rejects all positive metaphysics should become clear soon. It should however already be clear that it is a return to some sort of metaphysics.

Why did Nietzsche turn to philosophy? So far we can say that Nietzsche's primary concern was to find a value system for himself (so he probably would have understood philosophy as love of wisdom rather than love of the truth). Since value systems traditionally always have their ultimate justification in some sort of metaphysics, as one can see in the examples of Plato and Aristotle in the best way, it seems clear that he has to deal with the traditional questions of philosophy as well. In contrast to most of the thinkers prior to him he would have agreed with the analysis of what philosophers actually do which I gave earlier on. I have said earlier that a great philosopher has to have many special and consistent insights in the different branches of philosophy. Traditional philosophers might have agreed with this as well, but they would have added that the insights are related to either another world of eternal truth or the sense perceptions that all of us supposedly have in common. Both of these cases imply that the philosophy which comes out in the end must be the same for everyone who fulfils this task properly, e.g. there is only one truth and the true philosophy reveals it. This, however, is something Nietzsche denies. He takes into consideration how many philosophers have lived and how many different systems were brought about by them. This made him believe that all philosophies are contingent. However, as he would subscribe to the analysis of philosophy I have stated before, he realises that all philosophies have in common that they were created by human beings who are related in some way to what they have created. He denies that there is an absolute realm of knowledge, which is independent of its perceiver, whether it is the realm of physical objects or the realm of eternal truth. Whatever a person says or does always expresses something about the person in question. This is one of his basis insights. Because this is his position he also cannot and does not put his own views forward as the truth. He claims that all he says simply represents his own perspective, based on his own insights. Why does he put it forward then, if he just regards it as his perspective, one might wonder? He regards it as superior in some respect, but not with respect to the truth. He thinks that his perspective represents what the spirit of the times will make one think in the next centuries. This might sound very prophetic at the moment, but I will not clarify this point any further at this stage. As I have said before, the way in which Nietzsche replies to this question is what this book mainly is supposed to demonstrate.

So let me come back to Nietzsche's starting point. Although he is mainly concerned with values, he also has to deal with the other traditional questions of philosophy for the sake of justification of his values. After he realised the variety of philosophies in the world, he thought that there cannot be an absolute realm or objective external world to which all of these diverse thinkers have access, but that the expression of a philosophical view was always mainly influenced by the one who expressed it. The position was also held by Fichte who claimed that what philosophy one adopts depends upon what kind of person one is. Nietzsche always sees the wholeness of a person when referring to a philosopher because of his conception that all the different drives and aims in a person always have to interact with each other. The necessary conclusion given these observations is that the whole person is responsible for the philosophy a person creates. The whole person for him is what he calls the whole body because a human being, for him, is the person's body and nothing else. This is what he uses as the starting point for his philosophy.

Since Nietzsche regards the body as being responsible for bringing about whatever one thinks and does he calls the body the "great reason" and opposes it in this way to our intellect, which is our "small reason," according to him. This "great reason" is the basis for his philosophy[5]. He regards it as superior to the "small reason" of the intellect. The "latter [intellect] is a mere 'tool or toy' of the former [body]" [quoted in Parkes (1991): P. 214]. Yet, Nietzsche's understanding of the term "body" is very different from its normal meaning as is made clear in "Thus spoke Zarathustra" [Z 1 "On the despisers of the body"]:

> But the awakened, the enlightened man says: I am body entirely, and nothing beside; and soul is only something about the body.
>
> The body is a great reason, a multiplicity with one sense, a war and a peace, a herd and a herdsman.
>
> Your small reason, which you call spirit, is also a instrument of your body, a little instrument and toy of your great reason.
>
> You say 'I' and are proud of this word. But greater than this—although you will not believe it—is your body and its great reason, which does not say 'I' but does 'I.'

This statement goes directly against the western philosophical (rationalist) tradition prior to Nietzsche, thinkers who mostly despised the body. It was typical for the earlier thinkers to believe that the "I" is a non-physical entity which contains our reason or intellect, with which we can get to know the eternal truth about the world (Descartes).—In addition Nietzsche was not much interested in the empiricist tradition. However, his relationship to empiricism is not that easily categorised. This should become clearer in the main parts of this book.—Referring to the rationalist tradition he said [quoted in ed. Parkes (1991): P. 221; KSA Vol. 13, 14 (96)]: "Their insanity was that one could carry around

---

5 This way of thinking was taken up again by Peter Sloterdijk who stresses the importance of the whole body. [Sloterdijk (1983)]

a 'beautiful soul' in a misbegotten corpse." An even clearer characterisation of Nietzsche's approach to philosophy is given in the preface 2 of the "Gay Science":

> The unconscious disguise of philosophical needs under the cloaks of the objective, ideal, purely spiritual goes to frightening length—and often I have asked myself whether, taking a large view, philosophy has not been merely an interpretation of the body and a misunderstanding of the body. Behind the value judgements, which have hitherto guided the history of thought, there are concealed misunderstandings of the physical constitution—of individuals or classes or whole races.

Nietzsche later in his work did reject the thesis that the body was physical because then he held that everything is the will to power, but at the moment we can leave this point aside. To prove that the aforementioned approach actually turns up fairly often in Nietzsche I will cite a couple of more passages, in which he expresses his approach to philosophy fairly clearly:
Nietzsche maintains that the body is

> By far the richer phenomenon, affording much clearer observation" [quoted in Parkes (1991): P. 221; KSA Vol. 11, 40 (15)]
>
> It is therefore methodologically permissible to take the richer phenomenon as a key to the understanding of the poorer" [quoted in ed. Parkes (1991): P. 221]; KSA vol. 12, 2 (91)]
>
> The human body, in which the whole of the farthest and nearest past of all organic becoming again becomes vitally incarnate, through which and way beyond which an enormous inaudible river seems to flow: the body is a far more amazing idea than the old 'soul'" [quoted in ed. Parkes (1991): P. 222; KSA Vol. 11, 36 (35)]
>
> The entire development of the spirit is perhaps a matter of the body: it is the story—now becoming perceptible—of a higher's body shaping itself. The organic climbs up still higher levels." [quoted in ed. Parkes (1991): P. 222; KSA Vol. 10, 24 (20)]

Perhaps the clearest rejection of empiricism and rationalism is the following statement:

> Sense and spirit are instruments and toys: behind them still lies the Self. It rules and is also the I's ruler.

> Behind your thoughts and feelings, my brother, stands a mighty commander, an unknown sage—he is called Self. He lives in your body, he is your body." [Z 1 "On the Despisers of the Body"]

Another point which should be stressed in this respect is that he does not contradict himself when he claims that he is a psychologist and on other pages that he is a physiologist, because he believes that the opposition of body and soul is nearly completely abandoned [UP 168][6].

This is the reason why he can say that "Proper refutations are physiological—bodily—ones,—and so the setting aside of ways of thought" [KSA Vol. 11, 26 (316) PF] and also defend that :

> Never yet has a deeper world of insight revealed itself to daring travellers and adventurers: and the psychologist who in this fashion 'brings a sacrifice'—it is not the sacrifizio dell'intelletto, on the contrary!—will at least be entitled to demand in return that psychology shall again be recognized as the queen of the sciences, to serve and prepare for which the other sciences exist. For psychology is now once and again the road to the fundamental problems. [BGE 1, 23]

To summarise the argument so far:

Nietzsche realised that in different times and at different places different philosophies have been regarded as true.

This observation convinces him that none of these philosophies is true.

He explains the existence of the different philosophies by reference to the different types of human beings the philosophers who created them were.

The whole of a human being brings about their philosophy.

(Of course, he is not claiming that what the philosophers think was not at all influenced by the time they were living in)

---

6 Although Freud denies that he had read Nietzsche when he was young, he acknowledged the similarity of Nietzsche's insights to the discoveries of his own psychoanalysis [Storr (1989): P. 120].

At this point, I also wish to stress that Lou Andreas-Salome, to whom Nietzsche proposed when he was in his late thirties and who Nietzsche regarded as having a similar outlook onto the world as himself, later on became a close friend of Freud (he kept a picture of her in his study room until he died), a student of psychoanalysis, and a psychoanalyst. She was also acquainted with Tolstoy, and Rilke, to name only a few of her many famous friends.

The whole of a human being is its body.

The body brings about what philosophers regard as necessary. (This is also the reason Nietzsche uses ad hominem arguments and, in contrast to other philosophers, is justified in using them. What he does not do, however, is commit the genetic fallacy, i.e. he does not claim that he can disprove a theory by explaining how it came about. All he can do is to give reasons to show why his thoughts are so appealing.)

Nietzsche's body brought about his views, since they also apply to himself.

There are, however, certain significant problems raised by this approach which I want to explore in some detail at a later stage. In brief these are as follows:

Since no human being has a better justified perspective (because each human being has only one body), all philosophies are equally false with respect to "the truth."

Still it is clear that we do not regard all philosophies as equally false, because we could not survive if we did this (we could never make any decision), and therefore our bodies developed a certain faculty (the intellect), which provides us with a basis upon which we can create a hierarchy of philosophies.

Our intellect tells us that what is contradictory cannot be correct.

So what is least contradictory is regarded as the best philosophy. (Nietzsche thinks the scientific spirit (with the intellect) will govern the next centuries and this will make his philosophy inevitable. The past centuries, according to him, were governed by the religious spirit, which then served the body as a means to survival.)

These, however, are only principles of our intellect (principle of coherence, which enables us to survive, but which does not correspond to reality—given Nietzsche's definition of the truth, which I will describe in the main parts of the book).

The last part of this argument will be set out in much more detail in the main part of the book. The following couple of lines are intended simply to show how Nietzsche gets from the insights just mentioned to the thought that the world is the will to power. It is important to bear in mind that the Will to power is different from the will to life in Schopenhauer, because the will to life in Schopenhauer is a close approximation to the "thing itself" (the noumenon), but Nietzsche cannot make sense out of the expression "the thing itself," since all the things he is acquainted with stand in a relation to himself and therefore cannot be "the thing itself" or the "things themselves." From this he concludes that the apparent world, i.e. the world he is acquainted with, is the only possible and thus the only real world. This should become clearer in the section on the will to power:

Why does the body want to survive? Why did the body develop the intellect?

For only if the body survives can it be powerful and power is what the whole body is aiming for, according to Nietzsche. Everything which happens within the body aims for power.

There is a permanent power struggle between the different parts of the body, which are part of the body's struggle for power in the world.

A further insight, brought about by Nietzsche's own body, told him that his body is within the world (is a part of the world).[7]

From this he concludes that not only his body is will to power, but that the whole world is will to power and nothing else.[8]

However, he remains consistent with what he said before by holding that this insight again was brought about by his body[9] *and is therefore only his philosophy (However, he thinks this will be regarded as necessary during the next centuries, because it was created via the help of principles of the intellect, the decisive capacity in making a decision about what most human beings think about the world in the forthcoming centuries).*

With this background, I can now start to describe what the will to power is, according to Nietzsche, in the next chapter (the beginning of the first main part).

---

7 "Man, in his highest and most noble elements, belongs completely to nature and carries its strange dual character within himself." [HC 1 in KSA Vol. 1, P. 783-792, my translation]

"Will can naturally only have an effect on will not on anything else" [BGE 2, 36, my translation]

8 "Only where there is life is there also will; not will to life but—thus I teach you—will to power .... Thus life once taught me; and with this I shall yet solve the riddle of your heart, you who are wisest." [Z "On Self-Overcoming"]

9 "There was no psychology at all before me" [EH "Why I am a destiny," 6]

Apollo

1.

I have baptised this part Apollo with reference to Nietzsche's earliest work "The Birth of Tragedy" in which he described how through the union of the opposing forces, Apollo and Dionysos, tragedy was created. Apollo and Dionysos stand for the creative and the destructive force in a human being as well as in nature. However, Nietzsche alters his position in his mature works on these forces. Here, there is no need to go into more detail about what these forces stand for in the "Birth of Tragedy." The headings of my main parts are not meant to correspond exactly to the meanings Nietzsche attributed to them at the time. Still, the sense which they have in my book is closely related to Nietzsche's, and shortly I will spell out what they are supposed to mean. One should also bear in mind that Dionysos in Nietzsche's latest works is a synthesis[10] of Apollo and Dionysos from his earlier ones. Apollo in this book mainly refers to the outcome of the creative force in human beings irrespective of what is created. (It refers to ones own perspective or world-view). In our case the human being meant is Nietzsche. Dionysos mainly refers to the outcome of the destructive force in human beings irrespective of what is destroyed. (Here ones own perspective is taken just as one of many in the history of thought, irrespective of one's own special relation to it).

In this part I will describe the metaphysical side of Nietzsche's "artistic metaphysics," and in the next main part, I will be concerned with the artistic aspect itself. The notion that metaphysics is artistic implies that Nietzsche does not put it forward as "the truth." Metaphysics has to be read not in Nietzsche's sense of the word (as referring to a philosophy which postulates a real world, beyond the physical one), but meaning a description of the world, an ontology. I will show that Nietzsche does put forward an ontology in the literal sense of the word—the

10 In the „Birth of Tragedy" one finds a third force, which he referred to as Socrates. Socrates was connected with logic, reason and Christianity and was opposed to Apollo and Dionysos. Later on, Nietzsche revised his position with respect to logic and reason and integrated both of them in his own views, but he kept his antagonistic position with respect to Christianity.

only contrast to the traditional ontologies being that it is not referred to as the true one.

In the last section of the introduction I tried to justify why I am starting my book with Nietzsche's metaphysics. The last point I was dealing with then was that for Nietzsche "the world is will to power and nothing besides." This I have to clarify in the first section of this main part. This main part of the book is divided up into two sections: the first one deals with the will to power and the second one with the eternal recurrence. Both of these topics are essential for an understanding of what the world is like for Nietzsche. There is one main element of Nietzsche's metaphysics which I will leave out here, his view that a thing is nothing but the sum of its effects, because it is more useful for my purposes to deal with this in the section on truth and perspectivism in the second main part of the book.

1.1

1.1.1 Will to Power

There have been many philosophers who regarded the striving for power to be the basis of all human actions, and the ones in question are not limited to a certain period of time or area. This one can see from the following examples: Thrasymachos, Hobbes, Adler, Foucault. However, Nietzsche went further than them, for he held that the whole world is will to power [WP 1067]. What does this mean?

Firstly, I want to mention some other expressions which Nietzsche sometimes uses instead of will to power. The most important ones are "organic," "life," and "force." However, one must be careful here, because some of these notions are ambiguous in Nietzsche's work; he employs the notions "organic" and "life" in various ways. In this book they only concern me when they are predicated of the whole, e.g. that everything is alive and organic, because everything is will to power. There is at least one other meaning of "life" and "organic" to be found in Nietzsche which is used to distinguish things with the common mode of (what one normally understands as) nutrition from the ones without. Even nutrition has two meanings in Nietzsche; firstly, the normal meaning, and secondly a slightly altered one which applies to the whole world. Because I do not have the space to deal with all of the connotations of this word, I will restrict my discussion to the one relevant for my purposes and simply point to the fact that there is another meaning of the notion to be found in Nietzsche. The justification for what I have just said will come up when it is needed in every individual case.

I will use the different notions which are equivalent to the will to power to be able to collect the qualities claimed for the will to power and his justification for these claims. In this way we can slowly build up our understanding of the will to power. I will start with the qualities Nietzsche attributes to the will to power, when he talks about the "organic," then with the notion "life," and "force." After that, I will briefly discuss his justification of why these qualities have to be thought of in connection with the will to power.

1.1.2 The Organic

We usually divide the world into the organic and the inorganic. However, Nietzsche does not believe that this distinction makes much sense, because everything, according to him, is governed by the will to power: "—that the will to power is what governs the inorganic world as well—or rather that there is no inorganic world," [KSA Vol. 11, 34 (247), PF]

So one could say that for Nietzsche the whole world is organic. This does not imply that there is only one organism because this contradicts the assumption that the whole world is organic:

> An infinite Becoming is a contradiction in terms, as it would call for an ever increasing force, and where would that increase come from? What would it feed on, so as to leave a remainder? The supposition that the universe is an organism contradicts the nature of what is organic. [KSA Vol. 9, 11 (213), PF]

All we have to consider at the moment is that something organic is an organism and needs nutrition in some way. Yet, if we assumed that the whole world was one organism, this would contradict the assumption that it is an organic being, because it could not nourish itself. Nutrition is a function which needs an organism and something external to it with which the organism can nourish itself. So it cannot be that individual organisms grow together to the point where the whole world is one organism. There is something else we can infer from this aphorism, namely that Nietzsche applies his intellect to his thoughts and insights. If something is contradictory it cannot be correct for him. This seems to go against what he claims elsewhere:

> In the formation of reason, logic, the categories, it was need that was authoritative ... the utilitarian fact that only when we see things coarsely and made equal do they become calculable and usable for us ... The categories are 'truths' only in the sense that they are conditions of life for us ... The subjective compulsion not to contradict here is a biological compulsion ... But what naivetè to extract from this a proof that we are therewith in possession of a 'truth in itself'!—Not being able to contradict is proof of an incapacity, not of 'truth.' [WP 515]

Here he clearly says that not being able to contradict a statement does not show that something is true, but earlier he also said about a statement that it is "Nietzsche's truth," because the opposite claim would be contradictory. Here we already realise the apparent tension within his thought which needs to be resolved. As I said before what I am putting forward in Apollo is "his (Nietzsche's) truth." Of "Nietzsche's truth," Nietzsche does not claim that it is "the truth." He has got "Nietzsche's truth," because something stable is essential for ones own survival. We cannot survive if we take our own beliefs to be as valid as all the others in the history of thought. Historical awareness is not enough to resolve the issue. Apollo deals with what is stable (unhistorical) for Nietzsche, and Dionysos with his historical awareness. Apollo just contains "Nietzsche's truth." So far it seems that "Nietzsche's truth" is meant to and does appeal to the intellect, e.g. logic and the categories of reason, because he used the law of non contradiction to establish that even if (or because) the whole world is organic, it cannot be the case that the whole world is an organism. He has even given us one reason already why he wanted "Nietzsche's truth" to appeal to the intellect by saying that it is necessary for our survival, as he said before. Yet, this is not the essential point, as I will show in the last part of the book.

Which qualities does Nietzsche attribute to the world by saying that it is organic? "I take it for granted that every thing organic has memoryand a sort of mind [spirit]. Only the apparatus of it is so delicate that for us it seems to be non-existent." [KSA Vol. 11, 25 (403), PF]

So the whole world or rather all organic things have a memory and a mind and he also explains why it does not appear to us like this by holding that the apparatus in many cases is too little, so that *we* cannot perceive it. Memory is the "amount of experience of all organic life" [KSA vol. 11, 26 (94), my translation] There is no forgetting in the organic realm, only some sort of digestion of what was experienced [KSA vol. 11, 34

(167), my translation]. This means that everything a thing (an organism) was involved in is still contained in that thing. I will soon clarify what Nietzsche means when he refers to a thing (an organism). Yet, all organic things (all organisms, the whole world) not only have memory but also has some sort of mind. Nietzsche just wants to say that one has to attribute perception to all the objects in the world [KSA vol. 11, 35 (53), my translation]. I will soon explain why this has to be the case. The necessity of attributing the quality of a mind to the whole world makes his metaphysics appear to be very similar to Leibniz', Spinoza's or some panpsychic world view.[11] In addition to the two qualities of the organic world mentioned, Nietzsche thinks that "the organic process presupposes permanent interpretation" [WP 643]. I will dedicate a whole section to explain the process of interpretation.

1.1.3 Life & Force

Another way to refer to the "organic world" is to say "life." The whole world is living, is organic, is will to power. The notion "life" implies many characteristics, e.g. order (hierarchy), striving, growth:

> the order of rank, merely formulates the highest law of life. [AC 57]
>
> In order to understand what 'life' is, what kind of striving and tension life is, the formula must apply as well to trees and plants as to animals. [WP 704]
>
> It is part of the concept of living that it must grow—that it must extend its power and consequently incorporate alien forces. [WP 728]

Order (hierarchy), striving, tension, growth, is characteristic of life, and implies inequality between the different things. To live is to be will to power [Z "On Self Overcoming"; BGE, 1, 13; BGE 9, 259; WP 55; WP 254], so the inequality of things has to be seen with respect to their

11 C. G. Jung took up these notions from Nietzsche's philosophy, and combined them with Schopenhauer's Platonic forms. In this way, he formed his theory of the archetypes which are permanently changing, unlike the Platonic forms. I think that Nietzsche's metaphysics is the only one, which takes up central elements of Leibniz's metaphysics and develops them further. For a comparison of Nietzsche's and Leibniz' metaphysics see Poellner [Poellner (1995): P. 277], and for a study on Spinoza and Nietzsche see Wurtzer [Wurtzer (1975)].

power, combined with their will. That one is justified in distinguishing the will and the power becomes obvious in Nietzsche's work, where he talks about the will or power only; for example when he explains that a certain quanta of will corresponds to a quanta of force [GM 1,13]. This seems to imply that whenever he talks about force, he is talking only about the will as something seperate from its goal—power. This is not so, because in the "Will to Power" [WP 688] he equates force with the will to power. So, "force" again is an ambiguous notion which one must handle very carefully. Most of the time he uses force to talk about the will to power. For the time being I wish to leave the expression "will to power" again and focus on "force." "Force" and "space" are different expressions for the same thing [KSA Vol. 11, 26 (431), my translation][12] so that it is obviously senseless or rather contradictory to talk of "empty space." Nietzsche tells us even more about "force," e.g. the amount of force always remains constant, force is not infinite, force has only a certain number of possible properties:

> At one time, it was thought that to an infinite activity in time there pertained a force that was infinite and that no employment would use up. Now, the force is believed to be unvarying, and so not needing any more to be infinitely great. [KSA vol. 9, 11 (269), PF]
>
> we forbid ourselves the notion of an infinite force; it is incompatible with the concept 'force' [KSA vol. 9, 11 (345), PF]
>
> There have been infinitely many layers of force, but not infinitely different layers. That would presuppose an indeterminate force. Force has only a 'certain number' of possible properties. [KSA vol. 9, 11 (232), PF]

Human beings have to think that the whole amount of force always remains constant, and is finite, and force can appear only in certain amounts, Nietzsche claims. These characteristics will be very important in the next sub-part [1.2]. At the moment they confirm that Nietzsche's metaphysics appeals or is supposed to appeal to the intellect, because he regards it as inevitable for us to hold these positions.

What can we say so far?

---

12 "That 'force' and 'space' are merely two expressions and different perspectives of the same thing: that 'empty space' is a contradiction in terms, in the same way as 'absolute purpose' (in Kant), 'the thing in itself' (in Kant), 'infinite force', 'blind will.'" [KSA vol. 11, 26 (431), my translation]

For Nietzsche the world is organic, is life, is force, is the will to power. The qualities he attributes to the organic things or organisms which constitute the world (the whole world cannot be one organism, but it is completely organic, so it has to be constituted out of organisms) are as follows: organisms have a mind, memory, the ability to digest the memories, and interpretative capacities. The whole amount of force or will to power is finite and always remains the same; things in the world can only be constituted out of certain amounts of force; the relationships these things have among each other are relationships with respect to their strength; and the central notion which underlies all the other ones is will to power, of course. In addition to this there is no such thing as "empty space" [KSA Vol. 11, 26 (431), my translation], because the world is "will to power and nothing besides" and "will can only act upon will" [BGE 2,36].

We have already gained some understanding of Nietzsche's metaphysics. His justification for some of the qualities of will to power are still far from clear however and these I will turn to next.

These qualities fall under two separate categories of justification. They either follow by necessity from his initial insight that the world is will to power and organic, or they are justified logically—by means of the intellect. Let me start with the first category of justification.

Since the world is will to power, it is organic. This step does not need any further justification; it is just the way it is. But the world cannot be one organism; it has to consist of many organisms, each one willing for power. For the time being let us assume that each organism aims for the greatest power increase at any instant. To do this each organism has to fight the best suited opponent for this purpose. To find out which one the best suited one is, it has to estimate the strength of the other organisms. This process Nietzsche calls "interpretation." Therefore all organisms must have the quality of being able to interpret. To interpret or to estimate the strength of opponents an organism needs to perceive them. For this purpose it needs a mind. Therefore, Nietzsche had to hold that all organisms have a mind. Yet, a mind on its own is not sufficient for interpretation. An interpretation can only be made on a basis; this basis is constituted out of past experiences and ones own qualities (vaguely). This is one reason why organisms in Nietzsche's theory needed a memory. Nietzsche has a very broad understanding of memory, as not only containing the experiences one has had oneself, but also those from one's forefathers [BGE 264]. The relations between organisms, e.g. hierarchy, and the qualities within them, e.g. strife and growth, are derived from the principle of the will to power itself. Since the world is the "will to power and nothing besides" and that "will can only act upon will" [BGE 2, 36], there can be no such thing as empty space. From this short passage one can get an idea of Nietzsche's justification of some of the qualities of will to power.

Turning to the second category of justification, this concerns qualities justified by reference to the intellect rather than by direct reference to the will to power; in these cases, it would lead to a contradiction if one tried to reject them. The second category (intellect), is based upon the first category (will to power).

Firstly, we can mention the claim that "will can only act upon will." This also belongs in the first category, because it follows from the claim that everything is will to power. But it can also be justified on its own as appealing to the demands of one's intellect. Spinoza also used this claim. In him it can be found as a premise of his reductio ad absurdum argument which he, however, employed to show that there can be only one substance: P1 = Two substances can only interact if they have a quality in common. P2 = If they have a quality in common, their essence is identical as well. C = Therefore there can only be one substance. P1 and P2 imply that substances can only interact if their essence is identical, which in Nietzsche is expressed as "will can only act upon will." This premise in Nietzsche as well as in Spinoza brings about an ontology consisting of one kind of substance. Yet, the difference between them is that in Spinoza the substance is unified, whereas in Nietzsche it cannot be unified, but has to be multiple.[13] Since the phrase "will can only act upon will" can be taken as a self-evident statement, I think that it is justified to put it in the second category of justifications. Secondly, there is the claim that the overall amount of force or will to power always is the same—the preservation of force or will to power, which can also be regarded as self-evident. Thirdly, Nietzsche's remarks that the notion of force is incommensurable with the notion of infinity which appeals to the intellect, and the point that force can only appear in certain quanta is in agreement with modern physics, for according to modern physicists energy can only appear in a quantity which is the

13 In addition in Spinoza the amount of substance is unlimited, whereas in Nietzsche it is limited. This, however, is not relevant to the point in question.

integral multiple of the Planck constant. I will come back to this point in more detail in the next sub-part (1.2).

The second category of justification makes it clear that his theory is supposed to appeal to the intellect. Why this is necessary for him will be explained later. So far, we should only bear in mind Nietzsche's remark from earlier on, that what cannot be thought otherwise does not have to be "the truth." Nietzsche thinks that some things are necessary for us to think, because they are essential for our survival. Of course, the will to power is the basis for our drive for survival. In this way the second category follows from the first category, the basis of which can be traced back to the argument in section D. There I explained how Nietzsche got the insight that the world is will to power. The first category completely depends on this.

1.1.4 Will to Power
Power-Quanta & Power-Constellation

Having dealt with the qualities of the world mentioned in relation to the organic, life, and force, we can now turn to the "will to power" to get a better grasp of what have been referred to as "organisms" until now. How then can we imagine this will to power?

According to Grimm the will to power is discontinuous and "consists of discrete, separate power-quanta which differ from one another only quantitatively (i.e. in degree of power), qualities being derivative of these quantitative differences." [Grimm (1977): P. 3]. He cites some passages to support this interpretation:

> ... there is no will: there are treaty drafts of will that are constantly increasing or losing their power. [WP 715]
>
> My idea is that every specific body strives to become master over all space and to extend its force (-its will to power:) and to thrust back all that resists its extension. But it continually encounters similar efforts on the part of other bodies, and ends by coming to an arrangement ('union') with those of them that are sufficiently related to it:—thus they then conspire together for power. And the process goes on ... [WP 636]

Grimm is right that Nietzsche does not hold that there is one unified will, but he definitely holds that the power-quanta are not completely discrete and separate. Of course, each power-quanta is defined by reference to its focus[14], but its borders are not as clearly defined as Grimm claims, because they are permanently interacting with their surrounding. Nietzsche cannot have held a position compatible with Grimm's interpretation, because Nietzsche holds that there is no such thing as "empty space" [KSA Vol. 11, 26 (431), my translation], for "will can only act upon will" [BGE 2, 36], and therefore a power-quantum always has to interact with another one. However, there would have to be "empty space," if Grimm's theory was correct and the power-quanta were completely separate and discrete. Therefore, it should be clear that what Nietzsche had in mind was a continuum (like most of the traditional metaphysical systems), though, in his case it was modified around certain centres which are in a permanent struggle with each other. The radius of each centre is fairly clearly defined, yet there is a certain area at the outer end of the radius, where the interaction with the other power-quantum takes place, which is more or less determinate, depending on the strength of the surrounding power-quanta and the relation one has with them. If a power-quantum works together with surrounding power-quanta, if it is far superior to them, or if they are indifferent to it, then its borders will (in most cases) be fairly stable, because then the struggle between the power-quanta is at a minimum. However, if there are two hostile power-quanta fighting with each other, both being equally strong, then their borders will usually be less clear. Imagine two boxers fighting against each other, bleeding, losing their ear lobes, in contrast to a couple in love which would be an example for the prior case[15]. This will soon become clearer.

Grimm argues that for Nietzsche qualities are derived from the quantitative differences of power-quanta, because if the world is will to power then it seems there cannot be any qualitative difference between worldly things. But this analysis cannot be right. It should be remembered that will to power has a memory. Now we can enquire how the memory is distributed. If each power-quantum has a memory

---

14 Willens-Punktationen—trans. as power-quanta—seems to imply that the will to power is just at a point. This, however, is misleading. The notion just includes the reference to the will. The will of the organism is a point, but the power is structure around it, one could say. This point has most probably misled Grimm to his mistaken interpretation.

15 In Sun Tzu's "Art of War" [Tzu (1990)] one can find some of the possible relationships between powers. Many of Sun Tzu's insights can also be found in Nietzsche's work

of its own then there could be qualitative differences in will to power as well, in which case Grimm would not be right. I cannot find anything definite in Nietzsche on this topic, but one can infer what he probably would have to say. Each power-quantum has its particular experiences which it can keep in its memory. It does not seem possible that these experiences can be accessible to all power-quanta straight away, given Nietzsche's denial that the world can be one unified organism. Yet power quanta permanently react with each other and thereby exchange parts of their will to power, so that the accompanying memory is also being exchanged. From this we can infer that there should be some memories which are universal, but others which can only be found in certain regions and again others only in one particular power-quantum. This again suggests Grimm is wrong, because Nietzsche must have held that there are not only quantitative differences between power-quanta but also qualitative ones, since the different histories of the power-quanta and therewith the different contents of their memory must also have brought about different qualities. Thus Grimm's explanation for differences with respect to qualities does not seem right.

To get a better grasp of what will to power is, we should consider the following passages:

> And do you know what 'the world' is to me? ...a monster of energy, without beginning, without end; a firm, iron magnitude of force that does not grow bigger or smaller, that does not expend itself, but only transforms itself; as a whole of unalterable size ... set in a definite space as a definite force, and not a space that might be 'empty' here or there ... at the same time one and many, increasing here and at the same time decreasing there ... eternally changing ... out of the simplest forms striving toward the most complex ... and then returning home to the simple out of this abundance ... This world is the will to power—and nothing besides! And you yourselves are also this will to power—and nothing besides! [WP 1067]
>
> —There are no durable ultimate units, no atoms, no monads ... there is no will: there are treaty drafts of will that are constantly increasing or losing their power. [WP 715]

Because Nietzsche holds that everything is permanently undergoing change, he had to say that there are no ultimate lasting entities. Even power-quanta (*Willens-Punktationen*) are not eternal, for they can dissolve and come into existence, as he explicitly states [WP 715]. Although

Nietzsche rejects the concept of the Leibnizian monad with respect to stability, it must be acknowledged that Nietzsche's power-quanta have a lot in common with the Leibnizian monads. In the same way, as everything for Nietzsche is constituted out of power-quanta, everything for Leibniz is made out of monads (stones, plants, human beings ...) which implies that in both cases the world is organic, and monads as well as power-quanta have "perceptions," i.e. mental states, of which not all are conscious. Yet, one should not press the similarity too far, because in Leibniz all the monads have the same initial cause because they were created by God, whereas Nietzsche rejects the possibility that the world can be one organism, and in Leibniz the monads cannot interact with another, but are where they are, and perceive whatever they perceive due to a pre-established harmony, whereas in Nietzsche interactions among power-quanta, and perception actually takes place[16].

So far I dealt with the power-quantum which is an individual will to power. Now I briefly have to mention the "power-constellation" ("*Macht-konstellation*") or "organism" which is no longer a single power-quantum, but a collection of power-quanta. Grimm correctly said that "power-quanta arrange themselves into groups or ... power-constellations ... in order to collectively increase their individual power." [Grimm (1977): P. 4]. As I have said before, every power-quantum tries to maximally enhance its own power at each instant. If this can be done more effectively in a power-constellation, i.e. together with other power-quanta, then the individual power-quantum will take this option. "The unity which these power-groups display is analogous to that of a political federation in which each member is primarily concerned with furthering his own ends, but finds that his own ends are better accomplished by combining forces with others" [Grimm (1977): P. 4].

The question which comes to mind is whether each power-quantum in every moment tries to attain the greatest increase of power or whether power-quanta can refrain from aiming for the greatest increase at one moment in order to have a higher increase in the future?

It seems most likely that a single power-quantum always has to try to attain the greatest increase of power for itself at any moment, for it does not have the capacity to delay striving for power, because it cannot reflect about it very well. Yet, some significant sort of reflection takes place in higher, more complex power-constellations. In them one can

16 A detailed description of the relationship between Nietzsche's power-quanta, and Leibniz' monads was given by Abel [Abel (1998): P. 15-28].

find the phenomenon of consciousness which according to Nietzsche was developed in human beings to a very high degree. One can get a good understanding of the importance of such consciousness from Owen [1995].

It is mainly human beings (not excluding over-men) who have the capacity to strategically refrain from maximally increasing their power at every instant. Thus an athlete who is training 400 m sprints might run 400 m ten times. Unlike an unreflective power-quantum he will not always go full speed, not only because then he would not not even complete ten runs but because he knows that he will in the end achieve a higher overall increase of power. Only a power-constellation with a high enough degree of consciousness has such options.

1.1.5 Will to Power
Will & Power

After having dealt with the more general structures of the will to power, I can finally analyse the basic constituents of a power-quantum, namely will and power.

Each power-quantum is will to power and this means that it is will and power and it can never not be will and power. Nietzsche talks about the strength of a will and the amount of power separately, so I assume that one can make this distinction and deal with these two notions separately, although they cannot exist independently of each other [HAH I, 460; TI "Skirmishes of an Untimely Man" 14; GS 5, 347]. That this distinction is sensible can easily be grasped, if we consider the following example: Jim who was born in the slums of Harlem has got a very strong will. He is working hard at his ambition to become an influential drug dealer. Still, it is not very likely that one regards him as a very powerful person. Gordon, on the other hand, was born into a family in Beverly Hills and is listed in the Forbes 400 list every year. He was educated at the best schools and universities. Yet, he was always just about doing enough, so that he can get through. This seems to show that he does not have a very strong will. Yet, he is regarded as very powerful. These two examples show that the distinction between will and power is a sensible one. However, it is only an intuitive way of showing it. In order to elucidate the theory of the will to power in Nietzsche we have to be concerned with the concept of the will and the concept of power in Nietzsche's writings. This I shall do next.

What then is the concept of a will and the concept of power?

Before considering some longer passages in order to find an answer to this question, let me say this first. It seems clear that for some thing to be a power-quantum implies that it already has some power and that it has a will (this will does not have to be a unified one. It is only unified in the case of an individual power-quantum. In a power-constellation, there are always several wills which constitute the overall will). Each power-quantum at any instant has to have a certain amount of power and it also has to have a certain strength of will. And given this distinction, we can hold that the form of a power-quanta is its will and its content is its power. In one context [WP 715] he describes the will as a point and from what was said before we can infer that the power is somehow structured around that will. This we should only take as a metaphor and not a depiction. The will can be stronger or weaker, but there are only degrees of strength, no absolutes. The same applies to the amount of power a power-quanta can have [HAH 2, 67]. Now we can deal with the concepts of the will and the power.

1.1.6 Will

Still it is unclear what the strength of the will depends on. How can the strength of the will of a power-quanta increase and decrease?

> I also want to make asceticism natural again; in place of the aim of denial, the aim of strengthening; a gymnastics of the will; abstinence and periods of fasting of all kinds, in the most spiritual realm, too; ... One should even devize tests for one's strength in being able to keep one's word. [WP 915]

This passage shows that there is a certain rationality in the will. A will, of course, is always a will to something [KSA Vol. 9, 4 (310)]. If the will to X has been deprived of discharge for some time, it will be even stronger when it can actually act again. So one can educate or strengthen ones will to X, by making oneself not discharge it.

However, if one is deprived from ever discharging the will to X, then one has to attribute to X so little value that one no longer has the will to X. This process is perhaps best called sublimation, because the will itself does not vanish, it now simply has to find a different outlet. Under such reinterpretation an activity which one might not have valued before receives value. I merely wished to establish here that there can be a certain rationality in the will, and that the will can increase and decrease[17]. That a will is nothing eternal I have shown before [WP 715].

1.1.7 Power

What is to be seen as high power, according to Nietzsche? I will begin by making some distinctions in order to present Nietzsche's understanding of the highest power as clearly as possible. Firstly, that between external and internal power. External power depends upon the relation a power-quantum has with its environment. In the case of a hereditary aristocracy, for example, the only authority for someone's power is that he was born into a certain family; it has nothing to do with their personal qualities. Internal power, on the other hand, depends upon the abilities of the respective power-quantum. One might just possess these (e.g. a girl with a slim figure), but to keep and increase them one has to work at them (e.g. diets and exercise to keep and improve her figure).

External power clearly is independent of the strength of one's will (of course the strength of one's will can influence one's external power, but it does not have to). Internal power, however, is not independent of one's strength of will. The stronger one's will the more internal power one can gain.

The will to power in Nietzsche's account in the beginning aims for internal power. From a certain stage—once one feels as if one belongs to the strongest power-quanta—the will might turn to external power, but it does not have to. Internal power includes the possibility or even likelihood of external power, but does not ensure it. External power depends either on internal power or on one's origin, e.g. simply by belonging to a family with external power. Internal power is a capacity a body has, though this need not be obvious. For example someone might be a very quick logical thinker; but might hide this capacity in some social settings. It is completely different with external power. For example a son of the British Queen has immense external power, independent of his internal capacities.

Still one has to bear in mind that each power-quantum has some power, yet whether this is publicly recognised or not is a different ques-

17 The similarity to Freud's theory of sublimation has to be noted here, and the close resemblance to Spinoza's theory of passions cannot be overlooked either.

tion. Someone might know the names of players of all European football clubs. This does not normally count as a manifestation of great power. Yet, it might in some settings. At a football quiz in a pub this person might be able to answer the most difficult questions. In this setting, and probably only in this, his knowledge could count as a great power. At a job interview this ability no longer would count as a great power. This shows that not all abilities are equally recognised. Someone might have a strong will and have worked hard at some activity, without anyone recognising this ability as a great power. Thus a strong will does not necessarily lead to power.

The ability at which one works to enhance one's internal power has to be well chosen. There has to be an environment in which it counts as a power. In the best case this would have to be the whole world. (The difference between the notion "ability" and the notion "power" is that the latter one implies an evaluation, whereas the former does not, but simply describes an activity). Each power-quantum, of course, tries to become excellent at an activity, for which it is suitable and which is well regarded in an influential setting. Nietzsche also posits a concept of highest power which is an essential constituent of this book; its full significance will reveal itself only in the third main part of this book. He justifies this concept by reference to his theory of evolution. This would need a full scholarly interpretation and is beyond my book, but I will give it a brief outline below and then set out what the highest power is for Nietzsche. One has to bear in mind that the concept of the highest power in Nietzsche is valid only relative to the present time and the near future, a point taken up in main part three. Let me give a brief summary of Nietzsche's theory of evolution then, in order to clarify his concept of the highest power.

For Nietzsche struggles for power were originally decided according to the physical strength of competing organisms. Each organism is will to power and can be viewed from a physical and from a mental perspective and as more complex organisms evolved, more importance was attached to their mental perspective. Physical strength remained decisive in the case of "inhuman" [Owen (1995): P. 73] or animals. In an inhuman society the physically strong were able to do whatever they desired (the absolute masters), while the physically weak had to do whatever they were told (the slaves). The slaves who had a strong will could not discharge it outwardly so they turned inward. Their inwardness created consciousness, and with this the human race and recognition of the superiority of the masters, which in turn led to resentment of them. Since men would rather will nothingness than not will at all, this is what slaves with strong wills, the priests, did. They willed nothingness by inventing a "real world," which is distinct from this world of change and into which one will enter having died. According to the priests only people with a slavish lifestyle would be granted a blissful life in that real world. Those with a masterly lifestyle would have to suffer for ever in this after-world. The priests, of course, knew there was no such world, but they were also aware of the power of this theory, because they knew that only they had a consciousness of what goes on in souls or inside a person, whereas the masters did not. Upon acquaintance with these after-worldly theories the masters became frightened at the threat of everlasting torture. The priests were very convincing in their role, because after they developed an after-worldly theory all the slaves accepted their suffering willingly and happily fulfilled their tasks. This, of course, made them more convincing. Frightened, the masters with weak will even gave in straight away and became followers of this movement. After some time this slavish theory governed wide parts of the world. There no longer was a strict hierarchical system, but from now on everyone had an equal right in their societies. In this way everyone had to turn inwards in some respect which is the reason why Nietzsche regards human beings as sick animals (AC 3). No one was able to do as he pleased anymore. Everybody had more or less expanded consciousness—the stronger healthier ones as well as the weak ones (weak or strong with respect to their bodily capacities). Of course there have always been people who were closer to the old aristocratic system, but the new slavish one was usually superior. After a long period the former masters, the strong and healthy, also had a consciousness comparable to the former slaves. This made them realise what was done to them and how they sacrificed their abilities for nothing, an after-world which does not exist. So a new species had to come into existence, one with a consciousness as powerful as the dominant one, but instead of hoping for an after-worldly life, trying to achieve immanent goals and with that an immanent gratification. These are the over-human beings, who by working for a goal that can be achieved are healthier than sick humans whose aims are non-existent. This over-human species obviously is not a return to the old aristocratic society, but a further step in the evolution of the human race[18].

---

18 The similarity of Nietzsche's *Uebermensch* with respect to traditional

What Nietzsche puts forward as the highest power is what the over-human beings would have to achieve. That is the reason why this concept is only valid for a certain time. I will now set out the concept of what the highest power is, according to Nietzsche:

> To impose being upon becoming the character of being—that is the supreme will to power.
>
> Twofold falsification, on the part of the senses and of the spirit, to preserve a world of that which is, which abides, which is equivalent, etc.
>
> That everything recurs is the closest approximation of a world of becoming to a world of being:—high point of the meditation. [WP 617]

The best means to become the strongest is by creating a philosophy which turns the world of Becoming into a world of Being. The highest will to power is to establish a great world view of one's own. Primarily for the sake of values, as said before because philosophy is the love of wisdom [KSA Vol. 11, 25 (451)], but also because they need their ultimate grounding in a metaphysics. Yet, this procedure is only the highest will to power, not the highest feeling of power. To create such a world-view is only of instrumental value to achieving the highest feeling of power which is itself of intrinsic value. The person who performs these sort of deeds is the philosopher who creates a culture [BGE 6, 207] which means that he creates new forms [KSA Vol. 7, 19 (299)], and in this way also creates values [BGE 6, 21; GM 1, notes]. Philosophy is the most spiritual[19] will to power [BGE 1, 9], and if the most spiritual ones or their theories govern in the political sense, then we have reached the highest culture [HAH 1, 261]. Spirituality is the only possibility to become master of everything [KSA Vol. 11, 34 (131)], because spirit is the means to impose form on chaos [WP 658]. The most spiritual

---

values to Dostoevsky's overman, as represented in his "Crime and Punishment," are striking. Both believe they are justified in rejecting traditional morality, due to their superiority in comparison to most of mankind.

I will discuss Nietzsche's relationship to Darwin later in this book, and a short comparison of Nietzsche's and Hegel's philosophy of history follows in the appendix.

19 Spirit is the combination of the mental qualities and consciousness, which enables organisms to make evaluations and to form a perspective..

ones are also the strongest [AC 57] and only they can reach the highest feeling of power:

> The highest feeling of power and sureness finds expression in a grand style [TI 11, "Skirmishes of an Untimely Man"]
>
> The highest type: the classical ideal—as the expression of the well-constitutedness of all the chief instincts. Therein the highest style: the grand style. Expression of the 'will to power' itself. The instinct that is most feared dares to acknowledge itself. [WP 341]
>
> The classical style is essentially a representation of this calm, simplification, abbreviation, concentration—the highest feeling of power is concentrated in the classical type. [WP 799]
>
> To be classical, one must possess all the strong, seemingly contradictory gifts and desires—but in such a way that they go together beneath one yoke; [WP 848]
>
> To grasp what a coldness, lucidity, hardness is part of all 'classical' taste: logic above all, happiness in spirituality, 'three unities', concentration, hatred for feeling, heart, esprit, hatred for the manifold, uncertain, rambling, for intimations, as well as for the brief, pointed, pretty, good-natured. One should not play with artistic formulas: one should remodel life so that afterward it has to formulate itself ... [WP 849]
>
> Classical taste: this means will to simplification, strengthening, to visible happiness, to the terrible, the courage of psychological nakedness ... [WP 868]
>
> The will to power appears ... among the strongest, richest, most independent, most courageous, as 'love of mankind', of 'the people', of the gospel, of truth, God; as sympathy; 'self-sacrifice', etc.; as overpowering, bearing away with oneself, taking into one's service, as instinctive self-involvement with a great quantum of power to which one is able to give direction: the hero, the prophet, the Caesar, the savior, the shepherd; (-sexual love, too, belongs here: it desires to overpower, to take possession, and it appears as self-surrender. Fundamentally, it is only love of one's 'instrument', of one's 'steed'—the conviction that this or that belongs to one because one is in a position to use it). [WP 776]

I have said before that the process of creating necessities, a culture, and new forms is only a means to becoming the strongest. Yet once one has become the strongest, one does not stop enhancing one's powers, but can turn to different means of enhancing power, using ways unavailable when one was not so strong (If one had taken them then, one could always have blamed oneself that one only did so out of weakness). Using spirit to impose Being on Becoming, increases the internal power of one's spirit and eventually can produce a world-view which corresponds to the classic ideal of style, because one can then experience the highest feeling of power. Once such a world-view is created, one can continue trying to enhance one's internal power (not only with respect to one's spirit, but in whatever way the world-view demands), but one can also try to enhance one's external power, it just depends on what the world-view demands. Although the ideal of the classic style sets some restrictions on one's theory, I guess that there are still different versions possible.

I hope that this paragraph has made clear Nietzsche's concept of the highest feeling of power, how one can reach it, and what the qualities are it has to incorporate.

1.1.8 Interpretation[20]

We have found out that individual power-quanta can group together to form power-constellations, and we have also gained a better idea of what is meant by "will to power" by considering the concepts of will and power. We should bear in mind that a power-quantum, or a thing, an organism, a power-constellation is will to power, and never only will or only power.

Let us consider how change happens in Nietzsche's metaphysic. In this way we have to focus our attention on the concept of interpretation, for these two concepts are closely connected. One can get an intuitive understanding of this connection considering an example from the human world.

John, a student, has to hand in an essay the next day. His girl friend asks him to go out for dinner and friends want to go to a pub with him. John knows that if he does not complete the work he will be kicked out of college, because he had already received a written warning from the head of the department. However, he wants to stay in college and get his degree. In addition, he thinks that if his girl friend and his friends do not understand his reasons for not going out with them,

20 The importance "interpretation" had in Nietzsche's philosophy, as well as the way he dealt with interpretation, had a considerable influence on twentieth century hermeneutics. I also regard it as justified to refer to his perspectivism as a hermeneutical and an epistemological theory.

and get angry with him, then they are not people he wants to be close to. These considerations brought about John's decision to stay in and work at his essay.

John had to interpret the given situation and decide what was best for them. Now I have to show how the process of interpretation has to be seen more widely within Nietzsche's underlying theory of the will to power. Firstly, one has to bear in mind that every power-quantum is a perspective, and every perspective an interpretation. At every instant every power-quantum interprets and has to interpret its environment, so that it can act in such a way that it believes it will attain the best possible outcome for itself. How does this work?

Finally, we can understand why Nietzsche had to claim that he presupposes a mind and memory for everything [KSA Vol. 11, 25 (403)]. The mind is essential for every power-quantum to perceive its environment and memory is necessary for it to make a judgement about its environment. Both capacities are essential for an interpretation or a perspective. A judgement about the environment implies an evaluation, and this can only be made on a certain basis. The basis in these cases is provided by the memory, by comparison with past events, sometimes by automatic reactions which are age-old memories transformed into instincts. So a power-quantum perceives its environment via its mental capacities and makes a judgement about it via its memory. It will find stronger power-constellations, equally strong ones and weaker ones. A power-quantum sometimes has to take into consideration the overall strength of the other power-constellations, at other times only some particular abilities or even only one. To some power-constellations will it feel indifferent, to others hostile, and to others friendly. All of these evaluation turn up in degrees—hostility, superiority, inferiority can never be absolute.

After having judged the different relations it has to its surroundings, it acts so that its increase of power is expected to be the maximum possible (the main exceptions here are human beings, as mentioned before). Whether it actually is the best possible option chosen is a completely different matter, because the perspective of the individual power-quantum is restricted (to its location, its memory ...) and its judgement therefore subject to mistake. This applies to every judgement; whether another power-quantum is regarded as stronger, weaker or equally strong, depends upon what the power-quantum thinks the result of a fight against it would bring about. If it thinks that it will win, then it regards itself as stronger. If it expects to lose, then it regards itself as weaker. If it foresees a hard fight, then it regards the other as having as much strength as itself. Because we have come to know how such judgement of other power-constellations comes about, we can understand that what we desire is not the actual, unconditional superiority of oneself. There cannot be such a thing since it all depends on judgements and environments or circumstances only, but we will the feeling of power, as Nietzsche himself so often points out. The feeling of power is that according to our own interpretation of the world, we are justified in feeling ourselves superior to the other power-constellations (what Nietzsche put forward as the greatest power that appeals to his existence most. Still, the exact relation to his theory will only be clarified in main part three). One can explain the feelings of hatred, friendliness and indifference in a similar way as the feelings of superiority, inferiority and equality. So Nietzsche's will to power metaphysics offers a way of unifying the psychology of emotions[21]. If the other power-quantum aims for power in a completely different category than oneself, then one feels indifferent to it. If it tries to achieve power in the same category as oneself, then one feels competitive and hostile towards it. If it seems to offer oneself the chance to form a bond with it, in which one could gain more power, than one could on one's own, then one feels friendly towards it.

Here one can see the underlying rationality of action in the exchange between power-quanta. Yet, the evaluation of the respective situation solely depends on one's memory, one's self-estimation and the judgements formed on that basis in comparison to what one perceives in one's environment. If it compares itself with its environment with respect to the overall strength, then the overall strength is relevant for its current purposes (e.g. comparing the qualities of one's former girl friends). If the comparison is only made with respect to one or some qualities, then only these are or seem to be relevant (e.g. chess competition). This is the most general account of interpretation which I can give; for a more detailed description, one has to consider individual instances.

According to Nietzsche, a power-quantum is to be described as active, if it can act according to its primary choice, and a power-quantum is

21 This goes against Robert C. Solomon's claim in his book *The Passions: Emotions and the Meaning of Life* [Solomon (1993)] that there is no single principle by virtue of which we can explain the rationality of our emotions.

to be described as passive, if this does not happen, because it is being attacked by another power-quantum.

1.1.9 Thing = Sum of its Effects

So far we have spoken about power-quanta and power-constellations as if they were independent entities. Yet, now as we enter deeper into Nietzsche's metaphysics, we have to realise that for him a thing is never an independent entity. A thing, a power-constellation is always what it does, and what it does can be different with respect to different power-constellations. So the thing in the end for Nietzsche can only be defined by the sum of its effects it has on other power-constellations.

> A power-quantum is characterized by the effect it produces and it resists ... [quoted in Grimm (1977): P. 6; Nachlass Fruehjahr 1888, 14 [79], KGW VIII 3, 49 ff. ; PF]
>
> The properties of a thing are effects on other 'things.' Prescind from these, and no single thing will have any properties; that is, there is no one thing without other things; that is there is no 'thing in itself.' [quoted in Grimm (1977): P. 6; Nachlass, Herbst 1885-Herbst 1886, 2 [85]; KGW VIII 1,102; PF]

These observations clearly follow from what was said before and they are essential for his metaphysics, nevertheless I will not discuss this point at the moment, because it is more efficient to deal with this topic in the section on "truth." We can keep in mind that for Nietzsche a thing is only the sum of its effects, and that therefore a Kantian "thing itself" is counterintuitive.

1.1.10 Power, Pleasure & Pain

The following section deals with pleasure and pain and their relationship to the feeling of power. This might at first not seem to be relevant for an understanding of Nietzsche's metaphysics, but this is not correct. One has to bear in mind that, according to Nietzsche everything has a mind. Therefore everything has to be able to feel pleasure and pain in the same way that everything must be able to have the feeling of power, because everything is will to power and aims for a feeling of a superiority of power. In addition, this section makes us aware of the consequences the theory of the will to power has and is also relevant for an understanding of Nietzsche himself. Furthermore, this section provides an additional tool towards answering the question "Why does Nietzsche put forward his philosophy, if he does not regard it as absolutely true? ."

In the concluding paragraphs of this section, I will deal with the relationship between the will to power theory and hedonism, traditionally the main theory of motivation, declaring that we desire pleasure and try to avoid pain (which of these two strains was stressed more was different in every particular theory)[22]. Nietzsche offers a different theory of motivation which claims that all we desire is power, or more accurately the feeling of internal power. He does not deny that we can feel pain and pleasure, but that these are ever motives for our actions.

I will now try to explain how the notions of pain and pleasure are intertwined with the theory of the will to power. I will collect some passages and then show which standpoint Nietzsche takes:

> To exercise power costs efforts and demands courage. [HAH 2, 251]
>
> What is a pleasure but: an excitation of the feeling of power by an obstacle ... so it swells up. Thus all pleasure includes pain.—If the pleasure is to be very great, the pains must be very protracted and the tension of the bow tremendous. [WP 658]
>
> Pain is the feeling in face of an obstacle: But since we can be aware of power only in the face of obstacles, pain a necessary part of all activity—(every activity must be directed at something that has to be overcome). So the will to power also strives for resistance, for pain. There is a will to suffering at the root of all organic life. [KSA Vol. 11, 26 (275), PF]

All these excerpts tell us the same, namely that willing implies suffering. As long as something exists, it is will to power, and therefore wills something all the time. To gain what it wills, it has to overcome obstacles, which is painful. The more a thing or power-constellation wills, the more pain it has to be able to endure, yet the more pleasure it can gain in the end. However, it is not the pleasure we are aiming for, it is the power, according to Nietzsche.

22 Other theories of motivation were put forward by Schopenhauer, Darwin, and Freud. According to Darwin human beings are motivated by their desire to survive, Freud believed (at some stage of his career) that the sex drive was at the basis of all human actions, and Schopenhauer held that the will to life was the basic metaphysical drive.

> The measure of failure and fatality must grow with the resistance a force seeks to master; and as a force can expend itself only on what resists it, there is necessarily an ingredient of displeasure in every action. But this displeasure acts as a lure of life and strengthens the will to power. [WP 694]
>
> The decision about what arouses pleasure and what arouses displeasure depends upon the degree of power: something that in relation to small quantum of power appears dangerous and seems to require the speediest defence, can evoke, given the consciousness of greater power, a voluptuous excitation and a feeling of pleasure. [WP 669]

The last two paragraphs express the previous distinction between the different possibilities of relations between power-constellations. The stronger an opponent is, the more resistance one has to expect and together with this pain. In the case of human beings, one must not only think of another man as an opponent for one man, but rather a theory, or an ideal self which one has set for oneself, because the will to power primarily aims for internal power which one can only gain via the process of self-overcoming. If an opponent is weaker, then the fight will be easier, but the gain small. If the opponent is equally strong, then one can expect a very hard and long fight, but (possibly) also a very rewarding one. If the opponent is stronger, then one will lose. This is the reason why one fears stronger power-constellations. I have used stronger, weaker or equally strong in a general sense to refer to the overall power combined with the strength of will of the opponent. Who actually is stronger cannot be known with certainty by any of the opponents before the fight, but of course each power-constellation has a perspectival estimation of the strength of the other one, based on its own experiences, memory, world-interpretation, values and many other things. How exactly this perspectival estimation is constituted and what can be said about the differences between the apparent and the actual strength of the will and amount of power, can best be shown by some examples. I will not go into more detail about this here.

> there exists displeasure as a means of stimulating the increase of power, and displeasure following an overexpediture of power; in the first case a stimulus, in the second the result of an excessive stimulation. [WP 703]

The first case of pain we have already considered; it is the pain related to the strength of the opponent. The second sort of pain he is referring to in the last aphorism is the result of a fight with a stronger opponent. The temptation to fight it was too strong, but in the end it was unsuccessful. This obviously leads to pain which is either a result of willing, or of failing or losing against a stronger opponent, and there is probably also the case of simply feeling inferior which leads to the feeling of pain. Everything, however, aims for power; any feeling of pleasure is the consequence of this.

> Every animal ... instinctively strives for an optimum of favorable conditions under which it can expend all its strength and achieve its maximal feeling of power; [GM 3, 7]
>
> ...pleasure is a feeling of power. [WP 434]
>
> Pleasure appears where there is the feeling of power. [WP 1023]
>
> pleasure is only a symptom of the feeling of power attained, a consciousness of a difference. [WP 688]

Pleasure is only the feeling of superiority of ones own power. Perhaps it can also make itself felt, if one comes across a power-constellation whose abilities supplement one's own and with which one can enhance one's own power by co-operating with it in some way. I have not come across this case in his writings explicitly, but such a view does fit into his overall scheme, and is implicit in the comments he makes about friendship.

However, there are two comments which make me wonder whether Nietzsche himself was completely aware what his will to power theory would have to imply, because they seem to go against what was said before.

> Pleasure as the growth of feeling of power, which makes itself felt. [KSA Vol. 11, 27 (25), PF]
>
> Pleasure—any growth of power. Pain—any feeling that we are not able to resist, not able to become master. [quoted in Jaspers (1947): P. 300, PF]

If Nietzsche wants to say that we feel pleasure while we are fighting for the growth of our power, then I think this clearly goes against what he has said before, because while one power-constellation fights with another one the power-constellations have to experience some pain. I do not think that one can be consciously aware of pain and pleasure at the same time. They might both be present, yet one is always dominant. Yet, I think I know to which phenomenon Nietzsche was referring. Even while one is in the process of growth, one has to relax for some time; if one works at ones thesis, which is painful, one can gain temporary relaxation by looking out of the window and realising the feeling of the growth of ones insight/power/abilities. These brief periods of relaxation are the ones from which one gains pleasure. That Nietzsche refers to these brief periods of relaxation becomes obvious in the first of the last two citations which has to be read as such: "If the feeling of the increased power can make itself obvious, then a power-quantum or—constellation feels pleasure." It is not during the process of growth that one can experience pleasure, unless the process of growth demands so little attention that one at the same time can also be aware of one's own power which might enable one to feel enough pleasure to outweigh the pain of the fight one has to bear. Still, in this case I do not think that one is justified in calling what happens to oneself an actual process of growth. A significant growth can only happen against fairly strong opponents, this however implies that one has to be focused on the fight and will therefore only feel the pain which one has to overcome, due to the other being an obstacle for oneself.

Up to now, I have merely focused upon Nietzsche's metaphysics of the will to power. This has consequences on what he thinks about the future and the past of the world. I will deal with these in the next section.

1.2.

1.2.1 Eternal Recurrence of Everything

In this section I will put forward a metaphysical interpretation[23] of the "eternal recurrence of everything" (= ER), but I will not go through the

23 This type of interpretation has not been popular among Nietzsche scholars, for it seemed to them that the Eternal Recurrence of Everything is too absurd to be taken seriously. Yet, one should in this respect bear in mind another theory which implies perplexing claims—the Chaos theory. The creator of the Chaos Theory was the mathematician Henri Poincaré who was a contemporary of Nietzsche. The chaos theory describes irregular behaviours, and it shows that very simple recurrences produce very complex effects, which appear random, but are not.

ethical implications of this theory[24], for they are not relevant for the current purposes. Firstly, I will show how the theory of ER is linked to the theory of the will to power, and what ER stands for. At this stage, I shall also make a few comments about the plausibility of Nietzsche's justifications for his positions. Secondly, I will briefly discuss the relationship between the will to power and ER, and whether or not these two theories are contradictory or mutually exclusive, as has often been suggested. According to my interpretation, these two theories are not mutually exclusive, but depend on each other, and describe different aspects of Being. I am inclined to say that ER is the form of Being, whereas the will to power is its content. This shall become clearer soon.

1.2.2 From the Will to Power to the ER

In the following interpretation I will be extremely charitable to Nietzsche—perhaps too charitable for the taste of some people. I am well aware that the interpretation of ER which I will attribute to Nietzsche is not the only possible one, because one can find many attempted proofs in Nietzsche's unpublished notes which are simply inconclusive, because they contain a non sequitur. However, I have also come across unpublished notes which contain the premises needed to demonstrate what he wishes to establish. These provide me with good reasons to attribute the following interpretation to Nietzsche's thought; as I have said before I regard the application of Augustine's principle of charity to be necessary for a good interpretation. Where Nietzsche got these insights from and whether they appeal to one's intellect which is what he wants them to do, as we have seen the section on the will to power, is a separate question with which I will also be concerned.

In the first section of this part we have shown that the world is will to power and what this means. To complete his metaphysics Nietzsche had to wonder whether this world was created or not. This question did not trouble Nietzsche a lot, because he could not make sense out of the expression that something was created *ex nihilo*. "We need not worry about the hypothesis of a created world. The 'create' is today completely indefinable, unrealizable." [WP 1066]

This claim is fairly easy to understand, if one bears in mind Nietzsche's conception of the world. The world is will to power [WP 1067] and

24 A refreshing ethical interpretation of ER was given by Milan Kundera in his famous novel *The Unbearable Lightness of Being*.

will can only act upon will [BGE 2, 36], so how should will to power come into existence out of nothing? The will to power cannot have come into existence out of nothing. Therefore Nietzsche was able to rule out this option without hesitation. Yet, if the world was not created, it must have always been. The problem with this is that we do not seem to be able to make sense out of the notion "always," so how should this claim appeal to our intellect? "An infinite process cannot be conceived except as periodic." [KSA Vol. 10, 15 (18) PF]

Nietzsche had a seemingly appropriate reply to the aforementioned question. We cannot make sense out of the expression "infinite process" unless we think of the process in question as periodic. If the process was not periodic, we would have reached the end of an infinite series which clearly is a self-contradictory claim, at least it is meaningless and it does not appeal to one's intellect. Given his theory of the will to power and the demands of his intellect, Nietzsche had to hold that the world was never created and that it consists of a periodical process, an eternal cycle (a ring). If this was the line of thought taken by Nietzsche to reach ER theory, then I would regard it as an argument worthy of consideration, because he could have used this conclusion and then continued reasoning to think through which demands this makes on the claims of the will to power and the world. The history of the world repeats itself in certain periodical cycles, therefore the world has to be finite, and force can have only certain qualities.

Yet, in the previous section I alluded to how Nietzsche derived the theories that the amount of force is finite and that it can only have certain qualities; these were arguments contained in some of his aphorisms. He could have taken them and used them as premises for further enquiries, so that he reached ER theory via them. Given what I have written in section D, it should be clear that it is futile to argue which line of thought Nietzsche has taken, because what is important is that the initial insights of his theory are consistent; it is not the argument, but the insights that matter, and Nietzsche's insights are consistent. This is also the reason why there are several possibilities for setting out Nietzsche's philosophy.

That the history of the world repeats itself in periodical cycles is supported by the claims, which we have dealt with in the section on will to power—e.g. the amount of will to power is finite.

> At one time, it was thought that to an infinite activity in time there pertained a force that was infinite and that no employment would use up. Now the force is believed to be unvarying, and so not needing any more to be infinitely great. [KSA vol. 9, 11 (269), PF]
>
> We forbid ourselves the notion of an infinite force, it is incompatible with the concept 'force.' [KSA vol. 9, 11 (345), PF]

Nietzsche claimed that the amount of will to power is finite, because he regarded it as unthinkable that the world is infinite. Infinity has to be taken in the theological sense to include claims of unlimitedness, unboundedness, and being beyond the possibility of measure. In "The Philosophy in the Tragic Age of the Greek," Nietzsche already pointed out that this notion cannot apply to the world within our conceptual framework, because it is self-contradictory to hold that one has completed an infinite series: "Nothing infinite can exist: the result of such a supposition would be the contradictory concept of a completed infinity." [PTG 12 in KSA Vol. 1, 799 (873), PF]

So the rejection of the traditional understanding of infinity, which was being made in many sciences since the end of the 19th century, can already be found in Nietzsche. He used it to claim that the world can only be thought of as finite (and that time can only be regarded as cyclical, as I have said before). That the world is finite means that the sum total of energy in the world is finite. (If we accept that energy is force or will to power, for the time being). "There have been infinitely many layers of force, but not infinitely different layers; that would presuppose an indeterminate force. Force has only a 'certain number' of possible properties." [KSA Vol. 9, 11 (232), PF]

This citation clearly says that force can only have a limited number of possible qualities. It seems that he reached this insight in a similar way to the previous one. Given that we cannot make sense of the notion of "infinite amount of qualities," an expression which does not appeal to the intellect, he rejects its possibility, and holds that force can have only a finite amount of qualities. This might be thought to correspond to modern physical theory which holds that energy can only appear in a quantity which is the integral multiple of the Planck constant (Energy can only appear in a quantity = n * Planck constant; n = 1, 2, 3, ...). Of course, what Nietzsche says does not imply the exact Planck constant, but the consequences of this modern physical theory are that force only has a limited amount of qualities, if the whole amount of force is limited, a point which Nietzsche held. Nietzsche's theory as well as the modern physical theory turn out to have the same implications in the end. Modern physics, of course, has formulated it much more accurately, but does not contradict Nietzsche's statement. This last section also shows that Nietzsche had good reasons to hold that force has only a limited amount of properties or in exact terms: the total number of energy states in the universe is finite[25].

These premises together with Nietzsche's metaphysics justify his claim to the validity of ER. This is implicit in Nehamas remark that "in order to reach the conclusion that the history of the universe is eternally repeating itself, at least two premises are necessary

1: The sum total of energy in the world is finite
2: The total number of energy states in the universe is finite."
[Nehamas (1985): P. 143]

The phrase "at least" implies that even if both of these premises are given, it still depends on the ordering of the energy in question whether ER is necessary or not. Nehamas' claim can be made explicit in the following equation: ER = (1) + (2) + an appropriate metaphysics. Nietzsche held both of these premises and provided genuine reasons to believe in them, namely that we cannot comprehend an infinite amount of energy or an infinite number of energy states in the universe; in addition to this he held a metaphysics (WP) appropriate for ER.

Further premises necessary for the ER to occur are the following three: 3. Time and space must not be independent of energy. 4. The law governing the energy must be a determined one. 5. The reversibility of all states must be given. All of these premises Nietzsche implicitly or explicitly held. Premise 3 is implicit in Nietzsche's claim that there is only one type of substance, as will can only act upon will. The law

25 To attribute to Nietzsche an interpretation which has implications, similar to the ones held in modern physics might seem anachronistic, but one should bear in mind that firstly, many philosophies contain theories, which were later supported and justified through scientific research (the unconscious and Schopenhauer, perhaps already Spinoza or even Plato), and secondly I would also grant Aristotle a similar interpretation of the point in question, because he held that there is nothing "actually" infinite, but all infinity was solely "potential." I hope this clarifies my interpretation and renders it more appropriate and plausible.

which governs the energy, according to Nietzsche, is a determined one, which we can see at his WP theory. A determined law, as spelled out in the previous section, is part of his WP metaphysics. So premise 4 is also part of Nietzsche's metaphysics. In addition, there is nothing within Nietzsche's thinking which excludes the possibility of him having held premise 5.[26]

Therefore, I conclude that the will to power metaphysics is an appropriate philosophical framework because if one combines it with claims (1) and (2), ER follows by necessity. Since Nietzsche defended both premises by reference to the intellect, and justified the WP metaphysics by means of his insight combined with the use of the intellect, he is justified in calling ER the most scientific of hypotheses [WP 55]. Science, according to Nietzsche is built upon the structure of our intellect [HAH I, 19][27].

Simmel [(1995): P. 396-397] tried to show the two premises above are not enough to conclude ER, though this is not what Nietzsche claimed—an appropriate metaphysics is also necessary. However, due to the enormous influence of Simmel's argument, I feel obliged to show where it goes wrong. To disprove the two premises establish ER, he gives the following example, which is quite well stated in Kaufmann [(1974): P. 327]:

> Even if there were exceedingly few things in a finite space in a infinite time, they would not have to repeat the same configurations. Suppose there were three wheels of equal size, rotating on the same axis, one point marked on the circumference of each wheel, and these three points lined up in one straight line. If the second wheel rotated twice as fast as the first, and if the speed of the third was 1 / pi of the speed of the first, the initial line up would never recur.

26 I have been concerned with the ER in detail in the following two articles: Sorgner (2001a): P. 165-170 & Sorgner (2004b) , P. 169-188. In the first of these articles, I show that the concept of curved space by necessity is implicitly contained in the premises essential for the ER. Given premise 1 and 3, it follows that space has to curved. In the second article, I explain that all the premises necessary for the ER to occur are not contradicted by modern scientific research. It is even the case that many of the premises are directly supported by positions held in contemporary physics.

27 Interesting to note that in mathematics well behaved regularities can be captured in recursive definitions of infinity, which imply the recurrence of the same.

Simmel's rejection of ER seems to be an accepted position among many Nietzsche scholars. According to Nehamas, Soll remarks "that a random recombination of states might avoid Simmel's criticism, but rightly concludes that Nietzsche's determinism does not allow such an interpretation of recurrence" [Nehamas (1985): P. 248]. Soll is right to point out that Nietzsche's "determinism" does not allow recurrence to be interpreted as a random process. However, Simmel's refutation is wrong for different reasons. To what extent does it go against Nietzsche's proof of ER (at least the one I attributed to him)? The metaphysics which is implicit in Simmel's counter-example is not one Nietzsche could and would have accepted. In Nietzsche's will to power metaphysics there could not be any permanent absolutely constant speed, for everything which comes into existence has to vanish eventually. Simmel's counter-example, however, presupposes wheels which move at a constant speed for all time. Thus Simmel does not disprove Nietzsche reasoning for ER. Otherwise, Simmel is correct in most of his claims. Given his premises ER is indeed impossible because if part of a state of the world cannot repeat itself, the whole cannot recur either. The two premises in question are necessary for ER, but in addition the energy mentioned in them has to be ordered such that it does not exclude the possibility of ER. Nietzsche's will to power metaphysics is appropriate with the two premises it implies ER; the metaphysics in Simmel's so-called counter-example, however, already excludes the possibility of ER because part of the metaphysics cannot recur, and so the whole cannot recur either. So Simmel's counter-example does not work because he employs a metaphysics Nietzsche rejects (Actually, Simmel's metaphysics has implications hardly any sane person would want to hold, for it must leave one part of his universe in such a state that bodies can move at a perfectly constant speed for all times).

However, I was only able to attribute this argument to Nietzsche, because I applied the principle of charity to his texts. Actually, I was thinking that this is what a good interpreter does: He proposes the best possible theory which can be attributed to the philosopher in question. (Many interpreters do not do this, especially in the case of Nietzsche).

There are other arguments for ER in Nietzsche and most of them are pretty bad and invalid. However I have found passages out of which a rather good argument (mentioned above) could be reconstructed. For balance I will now show some of Nietzsche's bad arguments, and that this (most probably) indicates that Nietzsche was not entirely certain about how he should put the argument best or whether he could state it as a valid argument at all:

> The amount of force in the universe is determinate, nor anything 'infinite.' We must guard against such conceptual extravagances. And so the total of layers, changes, combinations and develoments of this force is enormous for practical purposes 'immeasurable'; but it is determinate and not infinite. To be sure, the time over which the universe exercises its force is infinite. That is, the force is ever the same and ever active; an infinity has already gone by before the present moment—that is, all possible developments must already have gone to pass. So the develoment here and now must be a repetition—so must the development that led to it, so must what comes from it, and so, forwards and backwards again. Everything has taken place countless times, in that the sum total of all dispositions of force recurs increasingly. [KSA Vol. 9, 11 (202), PF]

Here one can find the invalid inference from the above mentioned premise (1) to premise (2). Yet, it is clear that premise (1) does not imply premise (2) which Nehamas among others [Nehamas (1985): P. 144] has also pointed out. In addition to this Nietzsche was not using an appropriate terminology in this aphorism. The whole argument appears rather unclear, suggesting that Nietzsche's thinking was not too well organised on this topic. "The law of the conservation of energy demands eternal recurrence." [WP 1063]

In this phrase again an invalid inference was made. From the law of the conservation of energy alone one simply cannot infer ER; Nietzsche seems to have committed the same mistake as before. However, I do not want to go through the different mistakes in the several proofs of ER in Nietzsche. It seems to me to be enough to know that while Nietzsche's thinking about ER was not well ordered, one can find in his writings sufficient reasons to attribute to him the aforementioned interpretation of ER which renders his thinking on the matter consistent and is actually quite a fascinating theory.

1.2.3 Objections

Many interpreters doubt that ER was meant to be a cosmological principle at all. The most common reason for this is that in Nietzsche's published writings ER mostly appears in an ethical context. Nehamas points out that Nietzsche never published one of his proofs for ER [Nehamas (1985): P. 143]. This is correct, but does not imply that he has not held it. Most of his detailed metaphysical observations which show that he is the only one who further develops Leibniz' metaphysics can be found in his unpublished notes which also does not imply that he has not held them. He was clearly working on a metaphysical basis both for his remarks concerning power as well as for the ER. Thereby, I am not implying that his main work can be found in his unpublished notes. I am merely pointing out that metaphysical reflections occupied his thinking immensely, and that, therefore, the fact that he never published any of his proofs the ER does not imply that he did not regard the ER as a metaphysical theory.

Some might point out that Nietzsche himself rejects the cosmological interpretation of ER in the second of his "Untimely Meditations" [UM 2, 2] and therewith in his published work. This is correct, but one must bear in mind that the "Untimely Meditations" belong to his earlier works, and his philosophy changes significantly between his earlier and his later works. This applies most significantly to ER and to Nietzsche's attitude towards the intellect, e.g. logic and the faculties of reason. Many divergent statements can be found in the whole of Nietzsche's work, but one could not say that he had two completely antagonistic philosophies: the Apollinian and the Dionysian force are clearly part of his early as well as his late philosophy.

In one significant passage in Nietzsche's work which was ready for publication ("Ecce Homo"), he clearly says that ER is a cosmological theory, that he holds it to be true, and that it was probably already held in a similar form by Heraclitus and the Stoics:

> The doctrine of the 'eternal recurrence', that is, of the unconditional and infinitely repeated circular course of all things—this doctrine of Zarathustra might in the end have been taught already by Heraclitus. At least the Stoa has traces of it, and the Stoics inherited almost all of their principal notions from Heraclitus. [EH "The Birth of Tragedy," 3]

In "Thus spoke Zarathustra" one can also find clear statements which support the cosmological interpretation of ER which does not exclude the ethical one. e.g.:

> you are the teacher of the eternal recurrence—, that is your destiny! ... that all things recur eternally, and we ourselves, too; and that we have already existed an eternal number of times, and all things with us. You teach that there is a *great year of Becoming*, a monster of a great year, which must, like an hourglass, turn over again and again so that it may run down and run out again; [Z "The Convalescent"]

These two passages should provide me with enough support for my interpretation. One might say that I have not given the same sort of evidence with respect to the will to power of the first section of this main part, although there are interpreters who doubt that the will to power is a metaphysical theory. I did not do it, because for me the amount of material in Nietzsche's unpublished notes clearly suggests Nietzsche meant the WP as a metaphysical principle, in the sense I explained earlier on (e.g. WP 1067).

1.2.4 Is it self-contradictory to hold the WP & the ER theory?

There have been quite a few interpreters who have rejected any position which holds that the will to power and ER are consistent metaphysical theories. In Heidegger's work "Nietzsche" one can find the position of a couple of philosophers besides Heidegger himself who deal with this problem. In his "Nietzsche 1" [Heidegger (1961): Vol. 1, P. 30] he mentions Baeumler who held that the will to power was Nietzsche's main thought, but ER just his personal religious conviction. He tries to show the inconsistency of the two theories by putting forward the following argument:

> Will to power is Becoming; Being is grasped as Becoming; that is the ancient doctrine of Heraclitus on the flux of things and it is also Nietzsche's genuine teaching. His thought of eternal recurrence has to deny the unlimited flux of Becoming. The thought introduces a contradiction into Nietzsche's metaphysics. Therefore, either the doctrine of the will to power or that of eternal recurrence, only one of them, can define Nietzsche's philosophy. [Heidegger (1979): P. 22]

This shows, according to Baeumler, that the will to power and ER are contradictory theories. But is this correct? I do not think so, because for Baeumler becoming through the will to power implies that everything which follows has never been present before. This is linked to an infinity of time which is not cyclical, whereas Nietzsche regards the infinity of non cyclical time as unthinkable, and also regards creation *ex nihilo* as unthinkable. Therefore the only theory he is entitled to hold given his way of thinking is ER. In that case the will to power has to be incorrect according to Baeumler, because he regarded the will to power as a theory of permanent Becoming comparable to Heraclitus' which he interpreted as the permanent becoming of something which has never been before. According to Heidegger [Heidegger (1961): vol. 1, P. 30] this is not the best Heraclitus interpretation one can hold, because this sort of Becoming did not correspond to the Greek way of thinking. In addition, will to power and simple Becoming are not equivalent: Will to power is already an interpretation of Becoming, which is undetermined, and therefore is more than simple Becoming, because it already explains Becoming and gives Becoming determined features. One also should not forget that Nietzsche never did say explicitly that will to power implies that what has been cannot be again. He never claimed that the state which follows next is one which has never been here before. This gives us enough reasons to reject one premise of Baeumler's argument, namely that the will to power implies an infinity of new and different states of the universe.

The last interpretation of the relationship between the will to power and ER which I wish to mention is Heidegger's:

> If, on the contrary, we approach the matter in terms of the developed guiding questions, it becomes apparent that the word 'is' in these two major statements—being as a whole is will to power, and being as a whole is eternal recurrence of the same—in each case suggests something different. To say that being as a whole 'is' will to power means that being as such possesses the constitution of that which Nietzsche defines as will to power. And to say that being as a whole 'is' eternal recurrence of the same means that being as a whole is, as being, in the manner of eternal recurrence of the same. The determination 'will to power' replies to the question of being with respect to the latter's constitution; the determination 'eternal recurrence of the same' replies to the question of being with respect to its way to be. Yet constitution and manner of being do cohere as determinations of the beingness of beings. [Heidegger (1984): P. 199]

Here Heidegger tries to resolve the (apparent) tension between the theory of the will to power and the theory of ER by introducing a distinction. However, he does so with respect to *Seienden* (beings) and not to *Sein* (Being). He thinks that the will to power and ER are two modes of *Seienden* (beings). This, however, is not correct, for *Seiende* (beings) refers to something which is becoming or striving or changing. The will to power can be viewed as something *Seiendes* (beings), but only from the perspective of some sensible perception. From this perspective, however, ER is ontologically non existent; it belongs to the category of *Sein* (Being) and can only be grasped through the intellect. This can also be seen in the manner in which Nietzsche derived the theory of ER. The intellect tells us that ER can only be seen as a form which directs the history of the world. The ER being the great year, the ring, or the cycle, but always only the form which directs everything in it (I introduce this distinction to clarify the concept of ER). However, with respect to *Sein* (Being) the will to power is the history of the world, that which goes on inside the ring, the content. We can imagine *Sein* (Being) to be a ring constituted out of form and content which, of course, are inseparable from each other, in the same way in which the will to power and ER are inseparable. Heidegger introduced a similar distinction, but in his case he did not take this to be a distinction of *Sein* (Being), but of the *Seiendes* (beings). This however cannot be correct, for the following reasons. If we imagine *Sein* (Being) to be a ring, then this ring corresponds to the great year, or the whole history of the world which permanently recurs. Here we take an objective, external standpoint on the history of the world's being, a perspective the intellect enables us to have. We can only perceive *Seiendes* (beings) on the other hand, if we get inside the ring and take part in the action, the change, the striving, the will to power. But from this perspective we cannot grasp ER; the senses do not provide us with a knowledge of it. Therefore Heidegger's interpretation is mistaken, for he tried to take a perspective onto ER with respect to the *Seiendes* (beings), and this cannot be done.

With this discussion, I hope to have provided sufficient understanding for our purposes of ER as a metaphysical theory, and its relation to the will to power as a metaphysical theory. Both theories present Nietzsche's complete metaphysical philosophy, or one could say Nietzsche's ontology in the true sense of the word. Ontology meaning the teaching (*logos*) of Being (*Sein* or *ens*). The will to power being the content of Being, and ER the form. This insight completes the first main part of my book, Apollo, which aimed to present Nietzsche's metaphysics. The next main part is entitled Dionysos and will be concerned with the 'artistic' aspect of Nietzsche's metaphysics.

Dionysos

2.

After the foregoing reconstruction of Nietzsche's metaphysics, I can now turn to the destructive part of his thinking or to the "artistic" dimension of the "artistic metaphysics" Nietzsche created. "Artistic," because it does not claim to be true, and this also explains why his other theories are not true either, but what really stand behind them. That is what is destructive about this part and is the reason why I have entitled this chapter Dionysos. As I said before Dionysos stands for the destructive force; and this side of Nietzsche's thinking follows from his constructive one. My way of progression might appear to be a bit unusual—first having dealt with the constructive side, then with the destructive one. One usually thinks that first one has to destroy something, so that one can construct something new. This is correct, and this thought will play a main role in the third main part of this book, but for the sake of presentation I take the opposite line of thought, because I regard it as clearer. Now, I have to show how this side of Nietzsche's philosophy follows from his metaphysics. In the last main part "Apollo & Dionysos Reconciled" I will explain in detail how the destructive side of his philosophy does not in fact undermine the constructive one.

I will divide this main part of the book up into two subsections: the first entitled "Perspectivism & Truth" and the second "Nihilism." "Nihilism" represents the unavoidable consequences with respect to value judgements which follow from the observations of the first section. Only after I have dealt with all these topics, can I show clearly the apparent inconsistencies of Nietzsche's thought, and that they are not in fact inconsistent, but embedded in a consistent underlying philosophy.

2.1.

2.1.1 Perspectivism

I will begin this section by explaining how perspectivism follows from his metaphysics, outlining Nietzsche's understanding of perspectivism, and then discussing its relation to truth in all its various meanings in Nietzsche.

Perspectivism is the theory that "every view is an interpretation" [Nehamas (1985): P. 66].

How does perspectivism follow from Nietzsche's metaphysics? Firstly, some reminders from part one.

The world is "will to power and nothing besides." A single will to power is a power-quantum. Let us remember what a power-quantum consists of. In the centre of each power-quantum there is the will as a point, surrounded by power. These two constituents which never turn up on their own make up a power-quantum. Each power-quantum has a mind and memory. The mind enables it to perceive its environment, and the memory enables it to make value estimations. Individual power-quanta can group together and form power-constellations. Each of these power-quanta or power-constellations can be seen as an organism. Yet, there can never be an organism which consists of all the power-quanta presently in existence. The world can never be one organism. Each single power-quantum interprets its environment, that is, it has a perspective upon the world.

What does Nietzsche say about perspectivism?

> precisely this necessary perspectivism by virtue of which every center of force—and not only man—construes all the rest of the world from its own view-point, i.e., measures, feels, forms, according to its own force ... Perspectivism is only a complex form of specificity.—My idea is that every specific body strives to become master over all space and to extend its force (-its will to power:) and to thrust back all that resists its extension. But it continually encounters similar efforts on the part of other bodies, and ends by coming to an arrangement ('union') with those of them that are sufficiently related to it:—thus they then conspire together for power. And the process goes on ... [WP 636]

Here, Nietzsche describes the process I have referred to before, in the section on interpretation in main part one where he explains the purpose and the function of a perspective. Each power-quantum has its own view of the world and applies it to the actual perceptions it has in every single instant in order to be able to act respectively. "To act respectively" means that the power-quantum can attack another power-quantum, that it can attempt to unite itself with another one, or decide that the surrounding power-quanta are either too strong or too weak to use them for an enhancement of its own power. All this I have described in more detail in the section just mentioned. Now, I will try to elucidate the theory of perspectivism further from a variety of different angles.

What we have to bear in mind is that each power-quantum has a mind and a memory. Yet, a mind and memory can be employed in various ways. Let us try to get a clearer picture of what Nietzsche means.

2.1.2 Theories of Knowledge

Firstly, I wish to explain why perspectivism is not a theory of knowledge in the traditional sense of the word, this must be seen in connection with Nietzsche's rejection of the traditional theories of knowledge. Secondly, I wish to elucidate the theory of the non-existence of a subject in Nietzsche's conception. Then, I will briefly deal with the role of consciousness with respect to Nietzsche's perspectivism. After having dealt with these various aspects of perspectivism, I will mention the link between perspectivism and truth.

Let me start with the first point: Nietzsche's perspectivism is not a version of a traditional theory of knowledge. Traditional theories of knowledge are what they are, because they are regarded as enabling the person who applies them to grasp the truth as corresponding to the world. Empiricists base the principles of their knowledge on experience provided to us by the five senses, often referred to as sense-data, or the given (this is the information we get prior to any conceptualisation, or interpretation). Extreme rationalists base the principles of their knowledge on reason only. However, there are weaker versions of rationalism which hold that reason is merely a necessary constituent of knowledge. Yet, both empiricists as well as rationalists hold that their respective methods provide them with knowledge, and knowledge was usually linked to the truth in correspondence with the world. Nietzsche rejects both theories, and even the possibility of a theory of knowledge in general. How does he attack these two theories?

> Against positivism, which halts at phenomena—'There are only facts'—I would say: No, facts is precisely what there is not, only interpretations. We cannot establish any fact 'in itself': perhaps it is folly to want to do such a thing.
>
> 'Everything is subjective,' you say; but even this is interpretation. The 'subject' is not something given, it is something added and invented and projected behind what there is.—Finally, is it necessary to posit an interpreter behind the interpretation? Even this is invention, hypothesis.

> In so far as the word 'knowledge' has any meaning, the world is knowable; but it is intepretable otherwise, it has no meaning behing it, but countless meanings.—'Perspectivism.'
>
> It is our needs that interpret the world; our drives and their For and Against. Every drive is a kind of lust to rule; each one has its perspective that it would like to compel all the other drives to accept as a norm. [WP 481]
>
> Our perceptions, as we understand them: i.e., the sum of all those perceptions the becoming-conscious of which was useful and essential to us and to the entire organic process—therefore not all perceptions in general (e.g., not the electric); this means: we have senses only for a selection of our perceptions—those with which we have to concern ourselves in order to preserve ourselves. Consciousness is present only to the extent that consciousness is useful. It cannot be doubted that all sense perceptions are permeated with value judgements (useful and harmful—consequently, pleasant or unpleasant). Each individual color is also for us an expression of value (although we seldom admit it, or do so only after a protracted impression of exclusively the same color; e.g., a prisoner in prison, or a lunatic). Thus insects also react differently to different colors: some like [this color, some that]; e.g., the ants. [WP 505]
>
> there is an interpretations already in sense perceptions. [KSA Vol. 9, 10 (D 79), PF]

According to Nietzsche, all our sense perceptions are linked to experience of pain and pleasure (as well as value judgements, if we have values)—all power-quanta have perceptions—and because of this they can never be pure sense perceptions. Pure sense perceptions provide as us with data which corresponds to the objects. Yet, all sense perceptions are impure, according to Nietzsche, because they always are bound to include an interpretation and evaluation of the objects perceived. This interpretation, however, is made on the basis of who one is (the power-quantum or power-constellation one is). I wish to restrict the domain of power-constellations to human beings, because they are the ones relevant for this discussion. So the human being, who perceives the world never has a pure perception of the world, but is always restricted to his own interpretation of the world which is based upon typical features of human beings, like the intellect [WP 515], his own memory (as shown before), the memory of his ancestors [BGE 264], the culture in which he is brought up [KSA vol. 7, 19 (299); HAH 2, 188], his physiology [WP 676; KSA Vol. 11, 26 (316)], and even the language he uses

[TLN 1; WP 522; KSA vol. 9, 5 (45)]. One can explain this position at the following example:

A computer is never only a computer. For John, who studied computer sciences, the computer is essential for his survival. It is the object with which he spends most of his days. He knows how to give orders to the computer, so that it understands them and replies as it is expected of it. John loves Computers. Jim, on the other hand, hates computers. He used them in the past, when he tried to write his PhD thesis on one of them. However, just as he finished his PhD someone broke into his car and stole the backup disks of his thesis, as well as the copies he had printed out. At least I have got the thesis still on my hard Disk, Jim thought. He drove back home to print it out again, and to make new backup copies. Yet, when he turned on the computer he discovered that a virus has destroyed all his data. As a consequence of this, Jim lost all his material he had written for his PhD. He was so fed up that he never tried to rewrite it again. At the moment he is a taxi driver in London who hates computers.

This is an extreme example, of course, but Nietzsche thinks that this is the case for all our perceptions. It is no doubt that usually the values one attributes to perceptions are not as extreme as in this case, but one always sees perceptions in relation to our own feelings and values—the perceptions mean something to us. This does not only follow from Nietzsche's metaphysics, but also corresponds to our intuitions. It is also implicit in modern forms of interior architecture (Feng Shui), where the colours and the forms for a room are chosen on the basis of which form of stimulus is beneficial for the work which has to be done in the respective room. Even our common sense tells us that the colour red makes people aggressive. All these points are reasons in favour of Nietzsche's theory. My intention here is not to claim that Nietzsche is putting forward a compelling theory, but I regard it as the task of an interpreter to apply the principle of charity and to interpret the philosophy as strong as possible.

Since sense perceptions always imply an interpretation, they do not provide us with knowledge of the truth in correspondence with the world, but only with an interpretation of the world. A similar point was made by Richard Rorty who brought together Sellars' attack on the given, and in Quine's rejection of the analytic/synthetic distinction. Quine holds that every statement is subject to revision, even the law of non-contradiction. He observed that there cannot be a "neutral" synthetic observation, because every observation is infected by background assumptions, e.g. we perceive the world similarly to how our forefathers did, but we now longer hold that the world is stationary. From this he concluded: "The totality of our so-called knowledge or beliefs, from the most casual matters of geography and history to the profoundest laws of atomic physics or even of pure mathematics and logic is a man-made fabric which impinges on experience only at the edges." [Quine (1953)]. However, Rorty goes even further by combining this approach with Sellars attack on the given. Sellars introduces the distinction "knowing what x is like" and "knowing what sort of thing an x is." The first phrase implies only a pre-linguistic awareness, whereas the latter involves the ability to link the concept of a thing with other concepts so that one can justify claims about the first thing, e.g. it is a linguistic affair. However, if both of these claims are correct, then we have to conclude that knowledge does not even depend on experience on Quine's edges, because all we need for knowledge is to combine concepts together.

Rorty illustrates this as follows: "we can know what redness is like without knowing that it is different from blue, that it is a color, and so on. It is unnecessary because we can know all that, and a great deal more, about redness while having been blind from birth, and thus *not* knowing what redness is like. It is just false that we cannot talk and know about what we do not have raw feels of, and equally false that if we cannot talk about them we may nevertheless have justified true beliefs about them." [Rorty (1980): P. 184-185]. With this argument Rorty attacks empiricism as a basis for knowledge of the world. What is essential for Rorty [1989] is that all the concepts are merely contingent and together with this all languages. What we regard to be a truth is only a quality of linguistic creatures/systems. Since truth is a quality of sentences, the existence of sentences depends on a vocabulary, and a vocabulary is made by men, truth also is only man made. Men make these truths on the basis of what is useful for them. Rorty here agrees to the pragmatic definition of truth as put forward by William James. Thereby truth does not have an objective basis but only an ethical one. Rorty and Nietzsche agree in this respect. The difference between them is that Nietzsche gives an underlying analysis for James' statement about what is useful for men. Thereby he goes beyond Rorty. One might be tempted to argue at this stage that what Nietzsche puts forward as an underlying analysis of the respective phrase is only what is useful for

Nietzsche, but I will show in the third main part of the book that this is not the case in Nietzsche's conception.

The similarity between Nietzsche's and Rorty's arguments should show us the significance of Nietzsche as a thinker, given that Nietzsche wrote his theories a hundred years before Rorty. As a conclusion we can say that Nietzsche rejects empiricism as a theory with which we can grasp truth in correspondence with the world, because we can only interpret our environment, yet it is impossible for us and everything else to get a pure picture of our environment, for there is no such viewpoint.

Nietzsche's second attack on the theories of knowledge is his argument against the claim that rationalism can provide us with knowledge. I have alluded to this in main part one, and I will only say very little about it here, because I will treat it in depth in the section on truth. One of the most important aphorisms in this respect [WP 515] tells us that our inability to contradict the categories of reason and logic expresses only our inability, but not a truth. The reason why we are unable to contradict them is that only if we think within their categories we can have stability, and stability is necessary for our survival; our will to survive is an expression of our will to power. So if we apply these faculties then we should get a theory suitable for our survival, but not one which provides us with the truth. Therefore rationalism, as well as empiricism is not suited to be a theory of knowledge, because knowledge is always knowledge of the truth in correspondence with the world a position which we cannot achieve with either empiricism or rationalism.

These are Nietzsche's attacks on the traditional theories of knowledge, against which he puts forward his own perspectivism; however this is not a theory of knowledge, rather a theory which describes how everyone achieves their own apparent truths. Yet, I will come back to this point later in the section on truth. The next point I wish to discuss is Nietzsche's rejection of the standard picture of the subject which is closely inter-linked with his perspectivism.

2.1.3 Subject

> The assumption of one single subject is perhaps unnecessary; perhaps it is just as permissible to assume a multiplicity of subjects, whose interaction and struggle is the basis of our thought and our consciousness in general? A kind of aristocracy of 'cells' in which dominion resides? To be sure, an aristocracy of equals, used to ruling jointly

> and understanding how to command? My hypotheses: The subject as multiplicity. [WP 490]

The subject is a multiplicity, Nietzsche says, but what does this mean and why is this important for perspectivism? Again we have to bear in mind Nietzsche's metaphysics of the will to power, according to which human beings are power-constellations which are built out of many individual power-quanta. One can also refer to such a human being, or power-constellation as an organism which includes many smaller organisms and in the end individual power-quanta. Each power-quantum has its own interpretation of the world. The individual power-quanta gather together, if they think their individual goals can be enhanced in a better way in the shape of a power-constellations with other appropriate power-quanta. The respective power-constellations form new interpretations of the world which are built together out of all the different power-quanta. In this way the human-being also forms an individual perspective on the world, i.e. an interpretation of the world. However, the subject who forms this interpretation is not a unified subject, but is constituted out of a multiplicity of individual power-quanta. This is a point worth stressing, because the subject is usually seen as a unified self, most often "floating around" in a non-physical realm. However, there are also some other thinkers who agree with Nietzsche on that point. According to Hume, the "concept of the self has no empirical basis [Hume (1967): I. iv. 6]. All we need do, he says, is to look within: we will find "nothing but a bundle or collection of different perceptions" in a state of continual change. No single persisting thing over and above particular occurent perceptions can be discerned among them. It immediately follows, says Hume, that we are mistaken if we "suppose ourselves possessed of an invariable and uninterrupted existence through the whole course of our lives.'" [quoted in Grayling (1995): P. 540]. For Hume, the bundle of perceptions is kept together by resemblance, contiguity and causation, whereas in Nietzsche it is the organism, the links between the individual power-quanta which keeps the subject and its experiences linked together. In addition to this, the bundle of perceptions is kept together by our language, which presupposes a unified subject. A person is always referred to with the same name, although metaphysically there is nothing which justifies this habit.

Another thinker very familiar with the psyche held that the subject is not unified—Freud. I take psyche and subject to refer to the same entity. Freud distinguished different components of a psyche; he "considered mental life as produced by the interaction of three psychic agencies (Instanzen), the ego [Ich], the id [Es], and the superego [Ueber-Ich]. The ego was defined as 'the co-ordinated organisation of mental processes in a person.' There was a conscious and an unconscious part in the ego. To the conscious ego belonged perception and motor control, and to the unconscious ego, the dream censor and the process of repression. Language was an ego function; unconscious contents became preconscious through the medium of words. The id was ... the seat of both repressed material and the drives, to which had been added unconscious fantasies and unconscious feelings, notably feelings of guilt ... The superego is the watchful, judging, punishing agency in the individual, the source of social and religious feelings in mankind. Its origin was in the individual's former ego configuration which had been superseded, and above all in the introjection of the father figure as a part of the resolution of the Oedipus complex." [Ellenberger (1970): P. 515-516]. Besides the three psychic agencies, there is another—the ideal self (Ich Ideal). This should make it obvious that Nietzsche does not take an absurd and solitary position in that respect. One might even speculate that Nietzsche's "Genealogy of Morals" helped Freud to become aware of the superego. The last thinker I wish to mention concerning the concept of the subject is Wittgenstein. One does not usually think of him when one talks about the subject as a multiplicity. However, Wittgenstein does seem to hold that position in his Tractatus: "5.542 This shows too that there is no such thing as the souls—the subject, etc.—as it is conceived in the superficial psychology of the present day." [Wittgenstein (1961, 1974)].

The next point I wish to discuss about Nietzsche's philosophy is related to the last—it is consciousness. This is an even more mysterious topic. According to Nietzsche, every organism thinks continuously, but only a small part of this is done consciously, and therewith also verbally. The development of language and self consciousness go hand in hand, according to Nietzsche [GS 354]. Yet, we have consciousness only to such a degree as it is useful for us [WP 505]. If it is needed, an evolutionary process will take place to bring it about. This seems to imply that consciousness arises out of a need. So the more complex and detailed an interpretation of the world is written down in a book, the more aspects its author must have been in need of. This again provides Nietzsche with a justification to apply his *ad hominem* arguments to writers and thinkers, and it also gives us a new point of view of Nietzsche's perspectivism. In addition to this he developed a much more plausible version of consciousness, than Descartes, for example, who thought that all our "thinking is conscious."

After I have briefly dealt with the topics subject and consciousness with respect to perspectivism, I will come back to the initial topic—namely Nietzsche's attacks on the theories of knowledge of the truth as corresponding to the world. I wish to show why for Nietzsche it is not a shame that the theories of knowledge cannot provide us with any knowledge.

2.1.4 Value of Truth

Due to the close link between the will to power and perspectivism, we can understand why Nietzsche can hold that we do not desire truth for the truth's sake. He often claims:

> No, this bad taste, this will to truth, to 'truth by any price', this youthful madness in the love of the truth have lost their charm for us: for that we are too experienced, too serious, too gay, too burnt, too deep. [NCW Epilogue, 2]
>
> You think you are seeking 'the truth'? What you are looking for is a leader; you really want to get yourself put under order. [KSA vol. 10, 3 (1) 69, PF]
>
> The 'will to truth' develops itself in the service of the 'will to power.' Its proper task, if you look at it with precision, is to assist a certain kind of untruth to victory and endurance, to make a coherent mass of falsifications into the basis for the preservation of a particular kind of living creature. [KSA vol. 11, 43 (1), PF]

These aphorisms represent one of Nietzsche's most original ideas. He questions the value of the truth. In Plato the true, the good, and the beautiful are linked to another. In Nietzsche the truth is separated from the other two categories and even portrayed as something ugly which does not serve our survival. However, this is not a problem for him either, because human beings do not aim for the truth, but only for power. To claim that one possesses the truth can be a good means to gain power, since one still believes that the value of the truth cannot be doubted, but this does not render false the statement that we do not seek truth for the truth's sake. Nietzsche does not deny that men can have a will to truth, but the will to power underlies this will, and what we seek is not the truth, but an untruth, a falsification according to him. The will to power helps the will to truth to establish the victory of a certain untruth[28] because we cannot gain "the truth" and, as I will soon explain, it is essential for our survival that we are unable to do so. This is another reason for me to translate "philosophy" as love of wisdom in Nietzsche, and not as love of the truth, as I explained earlier.

So the will to truth is a will to establish a certain untruth for ourselves, a stable picture of the world which can serve as a basis for our actions in the world. Yet, every perspective is an interpretation, and it cannot provide us with "the truth." This is why Nietzsche calls perspectives which are essential for our survival perspectival falsifications. So a limited perspective, or rather a certain stupidity with respect to "the truth," is beneficial to our lives.

> perspective ..., the basic condition of all life. [BGE preface]
>
> synthetic judgements a priori should not 'be possible' at all: we have no right to them, in our mouths they are nothing but false judgements. But belief in their truth is, of course, necessary as foreground belief and ocular evidence belonging to the perspective optics of life. [BGE 1, 11]
>
> it is 'nature' in it ... which teaches the narrowing of perspective, and thus in a certain sense stupidity, as a condition of life and growth. [BGE 188]
>
> I put my finger on this vast perspectival falsification, by which the human species carries on. [KSA vol. 11, 43 (1), PF]

Here Nietzsche goes a step further than we have come so far. Firstly, I explained how in Nietzsche's metaphysics perspectives come about, and that they are interpretations of the world based on who one is. Now, he claims that it is necessary to have a perspective, an interpretation, and not "the truth," because only this enables us to cope with the world. Among the perspectives relevant for our survival, the synthetic a priori judgements which are made by the intellect are mentioned again; these are typical for all men, because they are essential for our survival. They are falsifications of the world, but beneficial ones with respect to our lives.

We have to realise that in many of these aphorisms Nietzsche is talking about a falsification when he describes perspectivism—a perspectival

28 We need *"truth,"* stability, or a leader on whose commands we can base our actions.

falsification or a false truth or even untruth. Yet, what does he mean by claiming that every perspective is false? If there is a false truth, should not there also be a true truth? At this point I will turn to the topic 'truth', because the claim that each perspective is a falsification or a false truth can only be understood if we know what truth means for Nietzsche.

2.1.5 "The Truth"

Truth in Nietzsche has a couple of different meanings. There is "Nietzsche's truth" (which is not be understood purely subjectively, as I already said. It is important to bear this in mind), "*truth*," "our truth" ('our' refers to the set of human beings), and "the truth." I will soon clarify these four different uses of the notion 'truth' in Nietzsche.

I will start with the notion "the truth," because this is the one he talks about when he says that each perspective is a false truth or that there are only perspectival falsifications. A closely related thought is expressed when one reads that there is no truth. The denial of the truth implies the theory of perspectival falsification, but goes beyond it by holding that there is no power-constellation and therewith organism which has "the truth." A perspectival falsification, for Nietzsche after all, is a condition for survival. All this will soon become clearer.

> There are many kinds of eyes. Even the sphinx has eyes—and consequently there are many kinds of 'truths', and consequently there is no truth. [WP 540]
>
> Henceforth, my dear philosophers, let us be on guard against the dangerous old conceptual fiction that posited a 'pure, will-less, painless, timeless knowing subject'; let us guard against the snares of such contradictory concepts as 'pure reason', 'absolute spirituality', 'knowledge in itself': these always demand that we should think of an eye that is completely unthinkable, an eye turned in no particular direction, in which the active and interpreting forces, through which alone seeing becomes seeing something, are supposed to be lacking; these always demand of the eye an absurdity and a nonsense. There is only a perspective seeing, only a perspective 'knowing'; and the more effects we allow to speak about one thing, the more eyes, different eyes, we can use to observe one thing, the more complete will our 'concept' of this thing, our 'objectivity' be. But to eliminate the will altogether, to suspend each and every affect, supposing we were capable of this—what would that mean but to castrate the intellect? [GM 3, 12]

Whenever he talks about "eyes" Nietzsche is referring to individual perspectives—either of a power-quantum or of a power-constellation. Each of these perspectives represents an interpretation of the world. Since there are many eyes or perspectives, there are many truths. And so Nietzsche concludes that there can be no absolute truth, but what does he mean by this?

This question is obviously related to the one I asked before when I was wondering what it means to say that every perspective falsifies. For there to be a truth, according to Nietzsche, there must be someone to have the truth, as we can infer from the last aphorism mentioned. Yet, no organism can possess knowledge of the world, because all the traditional theories of knowledge do not work, and his perspectivism provides every bearer of a perspective with a falsification of the world. The individual perspective is always brought about by the whole body or organism, and is therefore in the end caused by the will to power. Nothing is completely detached from the rest [Z "The drunken Song," 10]. As nothing is detached from anything else, everything also interacts with everything else, e.g. if we apply this awareness to human beings, we can conclude that there is no such drive in them as knowledge for knowledge's sake or art for art's sake. At the bottom of the will to creation and knowledge is the will to power, as is at the bottom of every other interest or action.

So every perspective is through one eye and it holds one interpretation of the world which was brought about in relation to its own interest and will to power. Each of these interpretations is a "*truth*," and because there are many such "*truths*," there is no "the truth." A "*truth*" is the individual perspective of a power-quantum or a power constellation. A power-constellation has a "*truth*" constituted as a mixture of the individual "*truths*" of its constituent power-quanta. What then could "the truth" be? The traditional understanding of "the truth" is abstractly expressed through the correspondence theory of truth. By means of reason and/or experience we used to believe we could gain access to an absolute realm of the Kantian things in themselves or Plato's true world as opposed to the apparent one. This procedure, it was believed, provided us with "the truth." Nietzsche, however, as we have just seen denies that we can achieve knowledge of the truth as correspondence to the world, and indeed has to do so given his metaphysics. He stresses this point very often:

> The 'real world', however one has hithero conceived it—it has always been the apparent world once again. [WP 566]
>
> The 'true world' and the 'apparent world'—that means: the mendaciously invented world and reality ... [EH Preface, 2]
>
> Overcoming of philosophers through the destruction of the world of being: intermediary period of nihilism: before there is yet present the strength to reverse values and to deify becoming and the apparent world as the only world, and to call them good. [WP 585]
>
> The history of an error
>
> 1. The true world—attainable for the sage, the pious, the virtuous man; he lives in it, he is it. (The oldest form of the idea, relatively sensible, simple, and persuasive. A cicumlocution for the sentence, 'I, Plato, am the truth.') ...
>
> 5. The 'true world'—an idea which is no longer good for anything, not even obligating—an idea which has become useless and superfluous—consequently, a refuted idea: let us abolish it! (Bright day; breakfast; return of bon sens and cheerfulness; Plato's embarrassed blush; pandemonium of all free spirits.)
>
> 6. The 'true world'—we have abolished. What world has remained? The apparent one perhaps? But no! With the true world we have also abolished the apparent one. (Noon; moment of the briefest shadow; end of the longest error; high point of humanity; Incipit Zarathustra.) [TI "How the 'true world' finally became a fable"]

Nietzsche refers to Plato's realm of forms or Kant's things in themselves when he mentions the real world, but these hypotheses are ill-founded. When Nietzsche talks about the apparent world, he means the world that we perceive with our five senses. Yet, he does not regard himself as justified anymore in referring to it as the apparent world, because "apparent" world implies that there is another real world, but this is not the case.

Since Nietzsche denies the real world beyond the appearances, he cannot have held the correspondence theory of truth in its traditional manner; his metaphysics is significantly different from traditional ones. But now the relationship between the apparent world, which in Nietzsche is no longer just apparent, and his definition of "the truth" needs to be explained. This will also clarify why Nietzsche does not regard himself as justified in calling the apparent world "apparent" anymore, and how it can be that according to Nietzsche there is nothing which appears.

Before finally being able to answer what "the truth" in Nietzsche means, I have to mention a part of Nietzsche's metaphysics which I have left out so far, but alluded to before in the section "A Thing is the Sum of its Effects."

> The properties of a thing are effects on other 'things'; if one removes other 'things', then a thing has no properties, i.e., there is no 'thing-in-itself.' [WP 557]
>
> The 'thing-in-itself' non sensical. If I remove all the relationships, all the 'properties', all the 'activities' of a thing, the thing does not remain over; because thingness has only been invented by us owing to the requirements of logic, thus with the aim of defining, communication (to bind together the multiplicity of relationships, properties, activities). [WP 558]
>
> 'Things that have a constitution in themselves'—a dogmatic idea with which one must break absolutely. [WP 559]
>
> That things possess a constitution in themselves quite apart from interpretation and subjectivity, is a quite idle hypothesis: it presupposes that interpretation and subjectivity are not essential, that a thing freed from all relationships would still be a thing. [WP 560]

A thing is nothing but the sum of the effects it produces on other things. We have said before that a thing is a power-quantum or a power-constellation[29]. According to Nietzsche's metaphysics, the paper lying in front of you with these words on it is a power-constellation. It has certain qualities, e.g. it has a certain size, it is mainly white, but it also contains some black signs which are the text. The paper is not very stiff, can be bent, ripped, and burned ... The description of course is not complete. In addition to the qualities it has on me which I did not mention, it has certain qualities for a caterpillar or a sea gull which are different to the ones I have attributed to it. Some qualities might even be similar. Yet, one cannot presume that how the world occurs to the sea gull and to me is similar. The entity I perceive as a paper might not exist as a separate entity for the sea gull at all. I wish to stress that entities such

---

29 One might be tempted to claim that one has discovered a clear inconsistency in Nietzsche's though at this point. On the one hand he claims that a thing is a power-constellation, which is constituted out of many power-quanta. A power-quanta being a point of will surrounded by power. On the other hand Nietzsche is holding that a thing is nothing but the sum of its effects. It can either be only the one or the other, one might be tempted to think. This is not the case. Every effect it produces is its power, which is driven by the will as a point.

as sea gulls, tables, and human beings having a perspective (in appropriate circumstances) on the paper is a feature of Nietzsche's metaphysics which is to a certain extent very similar to Leibniz's and which becomes obvious again at this point. What is important is that given Nietzsche's metaphysics even the table on which this paper is (probably) lying has got a certain perspective of this paper, because the power-constellation table also has "mental" qualities. The more perspectives of this paper another power-constellation has, the more objective [GM 3, 12] is its view of the thing. A thing, in our case the paper, is nothing but the effects it has on all other possible power-constellations (of which there is only a limited number, as I have argued in main part 1). Yet the perspective any of these individual objects has on the paper is bound to be a false perspective, because there have to be other perspectives which contain different qualities of the power-constellation. (Even the phrase "Different qualities of the power-constellation" shows how language leads us away from Nietzsche's world view, as he himself says. This sentence clearlyimplies that there is a thing which exists besides the qualities we can perceive of it. Nietzsche does not think that this is the case)[30].

30 According to Poellner [Poellner (1995): P. 284] the claim that a thing is nothing but the sum of its effects is incoherent: „it may be intelligible to say that this tree exists only as my 'idea', but I cannot also maintain that at the same time I exist only as an idea of some other mind or minds, and that other mind or minds in their turn exist only as an idea ('effect') in some yet further mind and so forth.

It is clear that on this interpretation of Nietzsche's anti-essentialism, which is the one most straightforwardly suggested by his explicit statements, we encounter an infinite regress. It is difficult to avoid the conclusion that if this is how we are to understand his assertion that nothing has a constitution in itself—i.e. that that notion is ultimately unintelligible—then this claim itself is an incoherent one."

I have to reply that the 'I' Poellner is talking about in Nietzsche is the whole body or organism, and that within a body there are many power-quanta who interact with one another. This interaction can be so intense, as in the case of a headache, that it becomes conscious. Yet, there is no consciousness seperate from the interacting forces which are part of a power-constellation. So the 'I' does not exist only as an idea of other minds, but the 'I' or rather the body exists as its effects on other things, plus the effects it has on itself. This, however, does not mean that there can be a 'thing in itself', because the body can effect itself, for it is constituted out of many power-quanta. One must not forget that a power-quantum per-

Why does a perspective have to be false? Because the whole universe cannot be one organism, for only if the whole universe was one organism all the time, then one could say that this organism has "the truth," because it would incorporate all possible perspectives on everything. However, since an organism can survive only if it nourishes itself with something external of itself, there cannot be such an organism and with it no truth. Here we can see that Nietzsche's conception of "the truth" again is some sort of God's eyes view, and his denial of "the truth" goes hand in hand with his famous claim that "God is dead" [GS 108]. "The truth" would comprise all possible perspectives on everything taken together—again this would bring in the correspondence theory of truth, but different from the traditional ones. Now, as we have got the concept of "the truth," it is even easier for us to explain what a thing is, given Nietzsche's metaphysics: the sum of all its effects. If we took away these effects, we would not be left with the thing in itself, but with nothing: "But I shall reiterate a hundred times that 'immediate certainty', like 'absolute knowledge' and 'thing in itself, contains a *contradictio in adjecto*: we really ought to get free from the seduction of words." [BGE 1, 16]

With the treatment of what things are, I have finally fulfilled what I promised in the first main section. I have also clarified what "the truth" stands for in Nietzsche's philosophy. Given these conceptions I can finally explain why every perspective is necessarily a false perspective, or why every perspective falsifies, although I think that the line of thought in that respect should already be obvious. "The truth" would be owned by an organism, if it united all possible perspectives of all times within itself. Therefore every organism which does not unite all possible perspectives of all times within itself, necessarily has to have a falsified perspective. Each of these falsified perspectives are "*truth*'s." They are the truths of the power-constellation or the organism who holds it. They are their way of interpreting the world, the basis for their actions. As I have said before, falsification is essential for survival which again serves the underlying will to power. One could not survive with "the truth," for "the truth" could not provide us a basis for our choices,

---

manently strives for power—it is the striving for power. Nietzsche's denial of the 'thing in itself' means that there cannot be just one power-quantum, analogously he denies that the world can be one organism. Power always implies a multiplicity, and thereby a power difference. This should answer the problem pointed out by Poellner, and make clear that Nietzsche's claim that a thing is nothing but the sum of its effects is not incoherent.

because it incorporates all perspectives. In addition "the truth" could only be reached, if the universe was, is and will always be only one organism and this is impossible, as I argued before.

2.1.6 "*Truth*" = A perspectival Falsification

What then can we say about individual perspectives? All of them are false with respect to "the truth," but are all of them equally false or are their differences in their degree of falsity?

Nietzsche held that the more perspectives of a thing are incorporated in ones point of view, the closer to "the truth" we get. It is, however, irrelevant for us how close we get to "the truth," because as I argued before we are not interested anyway in "the truth," there is no drive within us which aims for "the truth," for "the truth's" sake. We are aiming for power, and so is everything else. Our survival is in most cases a matter of gaining power, and our perspectives are false with respect to "the truth" so that we can survive. In addition to this, I think that we could not even decide which perspective incorporates the most perspectives, and is therewith closest to "the truth," because to be able to decide which perspective incorporates the most perspectives, one would have to know "the truth" with all its perspectives and one would have to be able to grasp all our own perspectives, and the ones of the power-constellation with whom one wants to compare one's perspective with respect to "the truth." This we cannot do, because as I said before our consciousness reduces the awareness of all our own perspectives to a level at which it is bearable for us. We are just conscious of a very limited amount of perspectives that we have. It is, of course, even harder to get to know how many perspectives another power-constellation has and can have on a thing. Due to this we are bound to say that all our perspectives are equally legitimate in respect of "the truth." We have to remain agnostics about the comparisons of our perspectives with respect to "the truth" within Nietzsche's metaphysics.

It might be replied that this is clearly false; we do compare perspectives and in many cases can clearly say which perspective is superior and which is inferior. And this reply might be strengthened by introducing a further distinction: We distinguish between explanatory quantity and explanatory quality. Explanatory quantity is how much a theory can explain. The Phillips curve in economics is a theory whose explanatory quantity is very small, because it has only a very limited field of application. The explanatory quantity of Aristotle's philosophy on the other hand is enormous. There are hardly any areas of life and the world Aristotle did not deal with. The explanatory quality deals with the content of the theory. The more contradictions a theory contains, the less valuable its explanatory quality. If a theory does not contain any contradictions, then the value of its explanatory quality has reached its maximum.

Whenever we compare perspectives with respect to "the truth," we consider the explanatory quality of a theory. In comparing two theories that which contains many internal contradictions is usually regarded as inferior with respect to "the truth" to one with less internal contradictions. Thus it might be said that we do have a basis on which to decide a hierarchy of perspectives.

Nietzsche would not deny that we have ways of ordering perspectives hierarchically, but he would reject that this says something about how the respective theories are related with respect to "the truth." We always have to remember:

> In the formation of reason, logic, the categories, it was need that was authoritative ... the utilitarian fact that only when we see things coarsely and made equal do they become calculable and usable for us ... The categories are 'truths' only in the sense that they are conditions of life for us ... The subjective compulsion not to contradict here is a biological compulsion ... But what naiveté to extract from this a proof that we are therewith in possession of a 'truth in itself'!—Not being able to contradict is proof of an incapacity, not of 'truth.' [WP 515]

It is the intellect with its logic and the categories of reason which enables us to create a hierarchy of perspectives. It does so not with respect to "the truth," but in order for us to survive:

> To what extent even our intellect is a consequence of conditions of existence—: we would not have it if we did not need to have it, and we would not have it as its is if we did not need to have it as it is, if we could live otherwise. [WP 498]

The intellect is necessary for us, and it is also essential that the intellect works the way it does. It could not be different from the way it is. Therefore the intellect in its current form is indispensable for us, and this is also the reason why Nietzsche's theory has to and does appeal to the intellect.

> As far as our own experiences go, we should always remain sceptical. For example, we ought to say that we can never claim an eternal validity for any 'law of nature'; that we can never claim a lasting persistence for any chemical quality. We are not subtle enough to detect the supposed absolute flux of events. What is persistent is there because of the coarseness of our organs, which manufacture unities and surfaces where in fact there is nothing of the sort. At every instant, a tree is something new; we assert its form because we cannot perceive the most delicate movement of it. We lay down a cross-section upon movement that is absolute; we impose lines and surfaces upon it, at the behest of the intellect. And that is the mistake—we presuppose equality and persistency, for we can see only what persists, and can recollect only what is similar [equal]. But reality itself is not so; we must not transfer our scepticism to the essence itself of things. [KSA vol. 9, 11 (293), PF]

Here Nietzsche explains how he thinks that the intellect functions. Since the permanent changes, the will to power, the struggle could not enable us to have any sense of stability, any stable concepts, anything certain or anything reliable, we could not survive while having Nietzsche's real world in our consciousness because human beings need stability and reliability. If a human being had nothing stable, but regarded everything as contingent and historical, then he would have to die, as I have tried to make plausible in D. Here the intellect comes in again. The intellect creates stability, similarity, concepts, pattern, forms, according to which we can structure our lives. They are delusory with respect to "the truth," of course, but they enable us to survive. Among the stability's the intellect has created are the categories of reason and logic.

> The inventive force that invented categories labored in the service of our needs, namely in our need for security, for quick understanding on the basis of signs and sounds, for means of abbreviation:—'substance', 'subject','object','being','becoming' have nothing to do with metaphysical truths.—It is the powerful who made the names of things to law, and among the powerful it is the greatest artist in abstraction who created the categories. [WP 513]
>
> Exactly the same thing could have happened with the categories of reason: they could have prevailed, after much groping and fumbling,

> through their relative utility—There came a point when one collected them together, raised them to consciousness as a whole,—and when one commanded them, i.e. when they had the effect of a command—From then on they counted as a priori, as beyond experience, as irrefutable. And yet they represent nothing more than the expediency of a certain race and species—their utility alone is their 'truth.' [WP 514]

The utility of the categories (causality ...) and the synthetic *a priori* judgements [BGE 1, 11] with respect to our survival (more accurately our will to power) makes them appear to us as unconditional truths. However, according to Nietzsche they are all no more than aids to our species for survival. They are "our truth," and we cannot help believing in them, because if we stop trusting them, we cease existing, and this goes against our will to power. It is in our interest to believe in what the intellect makes us believe in as a necessary truth, but which is only an aid to our species for survival. The same applies to our ideas of time and space, both of them are man made, as Nietzsche explains in the "Truth and Lies in the Extramoral Sense" [TLN end of 1 in KSA vol. 1, P. 873-890].

2.1.7 Logic

"Our truth" refers to everything the intellect makes us think of as necessary. This applies not only to the categories of reason and time and space, but also to logic.

> The conceptual ban of contradiction proceeds from the belief that we are able to form concepts, that the concept not only designates the essence of a thing but comprehends it—In fact, logic (like geometry and arithmetic) applies only to fictitious entities that we have created. Logic is an attempt to comprehend the actual world by means of a scheme of being posited by ourselves; more correctly, to make it formulatable and calculable for us. [WP 516]
>
> Logic itself as a consistent notation, build on developing the supposition that there are identical cases. [KSA vol. 11, 40 (27), PF]
>
> Logic too depends on presuppositions with which nothing in the real world corresponds, for example on the presupposition that there are identical things, that the same thing is identical at different points of time. [HAH 1, 11]

Logic functions in the same way the intellect does, for it is a part of it. Logic makes things calculable. In the case of logic we create identities without there being any—(this will become clear when I am discussing logic and language which I will do next). Given Nietzsche's metaphysics, there is no possibility of there being any two identical objects [HAH 1, 19]—Identity taken in the strongest Leibnizian sense (Leibniz's Law 'a = b iff all and only those predicates which are true of a are true of b' including predications as to spatiotemporal location)—, because a thing is the sum of its effects, and no two things can have the same 'locational' qualities (to stress this point. It is trivial given the above definition of Leibniz's Law), therefore it is impossible for two things to be absolutely identical. However, in logic we apply the notion of identity, as if two things actually could be identical. The argument Nietzsche puts forward to claim that logic and the law of non contradiction do not tell us anything about the world goes as follows:

A (universal) notion is a thought, description, proposition, or whatever, which applies to any case of a given kind.

The intellect presupposes that (universal) notions contain "the truth" (correspondence theory) about a thing.

Every (universal) notion (in the world of language) implies a concept and only that concept.

A concept (in the world of language) is made up of a certain limited amount of qualities (the ones essential to the universal notion).

"The truth" about a particular thing has to include all perspectives (qualities) of this thing (within one circle of the eternal recurrence).

However, a (universal) notion can never contain all the qualities of a particular thing, because it always includes only the essential qualities of the (universal) notion and can therefore never include all the qualities of the particular object which it would have to, if it was to bear "the truth" (correspondence theory) about that thing.

Therefore, the presupposition of the intellect, namely that (universal) notions contain "the truth" (correspondence theory) about a thing, is false with respect to "the truth."

Thereby, we can conclude that the intellect provides us with another falsified perspective of the world.

Of course, one might want to say that the very idea of a (universal) notion, i.e. one which applies to many, differing members of a kind, already means it does not cover all the qualities of each of the things it pertains. This implies that the above argument starts from a presumption that no philosopher has ever held, and to prove such a presumption false, as Nietzsche did, might appear to be silly. However, I do not think that it is as silly as it might appear to be, for what he wishes to say has some important implications for his understanding of "the truth." Since "the truth" about a thing implies all possible perspectives on that thing, a (universal) notion, however, only picks out certain qualities of this thing, "the truth" about a thing cannot be expressed via these notions, and this implies that "the truth" about any thing cannot be expressed in language at all, because it is in the nature of language to abstract with respect to the qualities of a thing. Therefore, even if the world was one organism (which it cannot be according to Nietzsche), "the truth" about this world could not be expressed by that organism in language, but could possibly just be experienced by that organism. So even if the argument goes against the presumption which no philosopher has ever held, it elucidates Nietzsche's high demands on what is needed to present "the truth," and it makes us question the possibility of presenting "the truth" about the world.

The above argument can be applied in various ways. For example we can apply it at numbers:

Numbers can be used for counting.

If one counts things, then one always has to use a notion which describes the various particular things in an abstract manner (e.g. 1, 2, 3 apples).

However, if we have to use abstract notions whenever we count things, then the sum of what we have counted can never tell us something about "the truth" (correspondence theory) about the world, because "the truth" (correspondence theory) about the world has to include the sum of all perspectives, yet by using abstract notions we only select some specific perspectives.

In case we take only a few selected perspectives of a thing, we have a falsified perspective ("*truth*").

Therefore whenever we employ numbers, we cannot expect to get "the truth." We can get a "*truth*" only.

The same principle can be applied at language in general as well, and Nietzsche does so, too. Language just creates another world, but it does not describe the world [HAH 1, 11]. Nietzsche does have a lot to say about language, but I will not be concerned with this topic in this book, because it is not of primary importance for my present concerns. All I wish to mention is the gap between perspectives which can be expressed via language, and the sum of perspectives which make up a thing. This remark should make it obvious that according to Nietzsche we can never express the truth (correspondence theory) about the world via language.

However, there is a reason why logic, language, and numbers only contain a very abstract and limited range of perspectives onto the world, namely the reason to survive. Only because we create these simple stable structures, can we get a basis for our actions. Logic and language make our life easier. This is their purpose, and it is no shame that they cannot provide us with "the truth," because we do not desire "the truth," but we desire power, and logic and language support that desire.

> Logic does not spring from will to truth. [WP 512]
>
> Logic was intended as faciliation; as a means of expression—not as truth—Later it acquired the effect of truth. [WP 538]

Here one can see again that logic as well as the categories of our intellect falsify the world, but are useful for our survival. Out of these falsifications, truths were created either by becoming essential constituents of our conceptualisation of the world, or by integrating them into our interpretations of the world. At the moment I am interested in the former, because we have already dealt with the latter.

2.1.8 "Our Truth"

> The most strongly believed *a priori* 'truths' are for me—provisional assumptions; e.g., the law of causality, a very well acquired habit of belief, so much a part of us that not to belive in it would destroy the race. But are they for that reason truths? What a conclusion! As if the preservation of man were a proof of truth! [WP 497]
>
> Truth is the kind of error without which a certain species of life could not live. The value for life is ultimately decisive. [WP 493]
>
> Ultimate skepsis.—What are man's truth's altimately? Merely his irrefutable errors. [GS 3, 265]
>
> The falseness of a judgement is to us not necessarily an objection to a judgement: it is here that our new language perhaps sounds strangest. The question is to what extent it is life-advancing, life-

> preservind, species-preserving, perhaps even species-breeding; and our fundamental tendency is to assert that the falsest judgements (to which synthetic judgements a priori belong) are the most indispensable to us, that without granting as true the fictions of logic, without measuring reality against the purely invented world of the unconditional and self-identical, without a continual falsification of the world by means of numbers, mankind could not live—that to renounce false judgements would be to renounce life, would be to deny life. To recognize untruth as a condition of life: that, to be sure, means to resist customary value-sentiments in a dangerous fashion; and a philosophy which ventures to do so places itself, by that act alone, beyond good and evil. [BGE 1, 4]

So "our truths" are simply our irrefutable mistakes, the necessities of our thinking (Intellect, logic, categories of reason, synthetic *a priori* judgements, categories of space and time ...). They are necessary, because without them the human race could not survive. I have talked about "*truth*" before when I was referring to the interpretations (falsifying perspectives) that power-constellations have of the world. "Our truth" is a sub-group of the group of "*truth*'s." "*Truth*" and "the truth" taken together constitute the notion 'truth.' "*Truth*" can never be "the truth." "*Truth*" necessarily falsifies. Therefore "our truth" also has to refer to a falsifying perspective.

The main question which arises now at this stage is the following: Nietzsche holds that every "*truth*," therefore also "our truth," necessarily presents a falsified perspective with respect to "the truth." In addition to this it is necessary for the perspective to be false with respect to "the truth," because we could not survive with "the truth," for it could not give us a determinate interpretation by which we could live. What now are we to make out of Nietzsche's own philosophy? If he claimed it to be "the truth," then he would contradict himself, yet contradictions do not appeal to our intellect, and in addition to this he would be doing something which endangers the human race, because falsification is essential for it, as he claimed before. Can this be Nietzsche's position after all he has said about the importance of logic and stability as a means for our survival? His philosophy is meant to be life enhancing, but this clearly would not be the case if he was putting forward "the truth," because men could not bear "the truth" and cannot reach it anyway.

This cannot be what Nietzsche meant, because in that case he would never have been considered the important thinker he is. In addition to this Nietzsche himself says that this is the wrong way to interpret him.

> —an interpreter who could bring before your eyes the universality and unconditionality of all 'will to power' in such a way that almost any word and even the word 'tyranny' would finally seem unsuitable or as a weakening and moderating metaphor—as too human—and who none the less ended by asserting of this world the same as you assert of it, namely that it has a 'necessary' and 'calculable' course, but not because laws prevail in it but because laws are absolutely lacking, and every power draws its ultimate consequences every moment. Granted this too is only interpretation—and you will be eager enough to raise this objection?—well, so much the better. [BGE 1, 22]

So Nietzsche remains consistent with his prior claims. Everything he says is also a falsifying perspective. It is a "*truth*." Nietzsche being a human being also has to stick to the laws of our species and take into consideration what we need for our survival, namely the intellect and this he does. So "Nietzsche's truth" incorporates or includes "our truth" which is a sub group of all "*truth's*" which is always a perspectival falsification and opposed to "the truth." This should have clarified the different meanings of truth in Nietzsche, his understanding of perspectivism and the place of his own philosophy with respect to all these claims. Still the most important question is left unanswered: Why should we believe Nietzsche, if he himself says that what he says is a perspectival falsification, and therewith false with respect to "the truth"? I will not answer this now, because the whole main part three is reserved for this purpose. Before I can answer the last question, I will have to deal with some other topics which concern some consequences of this chapter, namely nihilism. This will be the focus of the next and last section of this main part (Dionysos).

2.2.

2.2.1 Nihilism

The topic of this section follows directly from the denial of "the truth" in the last section, for nihilism is the view that there is no justification for any absolute standard. It is therefore closely related to such views as relativism. The relationship between nihilism and relativism is as follows: relativism claims that there is no eternal justification for an absolute standard, and that the standards which one can find in a certain domain are based upon the criteria which are presently relevant within this domain. This implies that it is possible that all criteria are subject to change. Nihilism holds that there is no justification for any absolute standard. So relativism implies nihilism, but not vice versa. This type of nihilism can turn up in a stronger and weaker form—the stronger one defending nihilism on a metaphysical level, the weaker one on an epistemological level. The weaker version of nihilism leaves open the possibility that there are absolute standards with respect to metaphysics (i.e. a set of absolute values might exist, but I cannot become aware of it), whereas the stronger version denies this possibility. In both cases a nihilist has to believe in nothing. It is, however, questionable, whether this traditional definition of nihilism is at all possible—in practice and in theory. It might be the case that this is a variant of the liar paradox:

> A says: I am a nihilist.
> This means: I believe in nothing—that there is no justification for any absolute standard.
> However, if A believes that there is no justification for any absolute standard, then he does believe in an absolute standard, namely the absolute standard that there is no absolute standard.
> This is a self-defeating position.

To me it seems that this is a good objection to nihilism as defined above. Yet, Nietzsche's understanding of nihilism is significantly different and does not suffer from the defects of the above mentioned definition. However, it seems to me as if many Anglo-American Nietzsche interpretations neglect his concept of nihilism. This attitude towards nihilism has to be sharply contrasted with the relevance continental thinkers attributed to nihilism, for example Heidegger, Sloterdijk, Camus were deeply affected by this topic, to mention only a few. My position is that an understanding of Nietzsche's nihilism is essential for an understanding of his philosophy as a whole. This position, I hope, will be made clear at the end of this book.

One has to bear in mind that nihilism, as well as truth in the previous chapter, has several different meanings for Nietzsche. I will distinguish three different conceptions of nihilism, to which I attach the following names: Schopenhauer's nihilism, Plato's nihilism, and Nietzsche's nihilism. I will be mainly concerned with the last type, which I will later on divide into active and passive nihilism to reveal the significance of this form of nihilism for Nietzsche's metaphysics and his philosophy of history. In addition to this, this form of nihilism is the one which is directly related to the previous chapter, for nihilism is directly linked to the loss of "the truth," whereas the other two concepts are not directly related to what I have been discussing so far. The importance of the other two concepts with respect to this book is rather limited, and therefore my treatment of them will be rather short.

With Nietzsche, "nihilism becomes conscious for the first time," according to Camus. [Camus (1962): P. 57] This praise alone should provide one with enough reason to deal with nihilism as a general theme in Nietzsche's work. The statement, however, is not supposed to mean that there was no idea of nihilism in life or thought before Nietzsche, but that Nietzsche was the first to characterise the concept clearly in its many varieties. Yet, there were other nihilists before him; it is arguable that Protagoras' relativism was one of the first nihilistic theories in philosophy. Yet, I do not wish to deal with the history of nihilism, but would like to make some further comments on the history of the word 'nihilism.' The word 'nihiliste' was used for example in the French Revolution to refer to an attitude of political and religious indifference. In philosophical discourse it was probably first used in a letter to Fichte by F. H. Jakobi (1799) who refers to the idealism of the former. From then on the notion of nihilism is significant in various respects. It was employed to refer to the French socialist movement of the nineteenth century as well as to the Left Wing Hegelians who inherited the accusation of being nihilistic from its idealistic predecessors Fichte, Schelling, and Hegel. These critical uses effect the transmissions of the word in the Russian political and social culture, from where they influenced Western Europe again. Especially in the great Russian novelists of the nineteenth century the concept of nihilism can be found in various manners. It is common practice to ascribe the invention of the notion "nihilism" to Turgenev who employed it to refer to young rebels in Tsarist Russia. Even Robert Solomon makes this mistake in his definition of "nihilism" in "The Oxford Companion to Philosophy" [Solomon (1995): P. 623].

Müller-Lauter [(1971): P. 66] shows that Turgenev was not even the first author in Russia who used this word.

In the last section I discussed truth and perspectivism in Nietzsche. There I established that Nietzsche thought that no power-constellation can have "the truth," but that each of the power-constellations has a "*truth*" which is necessarily false with respect to "the truth." Nietzsche reached this position by carefully thinking through his metaphysics of the will to power. "Thinking through what the will to power implies" means that he was using his intellect to make logical inferences from his initial premise that the world is will to power. The intellect then told him that what follows is that everything what was taken to be "the truth" is just a "*truth*" which is necessarily different from "the truth." The worldviews which have been taken to be "the truth" usually also provided people with an absolute foundation for their values. Due to this foundation the values were eternally and universally valid, that is, valid everywhere and at every time. With the loss of all these absolutes, human beings also got rid of the absolute foundation for their values. The denial of "the truth" or in other terms the loss of God brings nihilism along with it and this means: "the radical repudiation of value, meaning, and desirability" [WP 1]. "What does nihilism mean?—That the highest values devaluate themselves. The aim is lacking; 'why?' finds no answer." [WP 2]

However, if for Nietzsche this was what nihilism was all about, then his conception would not be different from the common sense understanding of the term. Yet, this is not the whole of Nietzsche's conception. Nihilism in Nietzsche is always part of a process of change. It is the result of something and brings about something new.

> Overcoming of philosophers through the destruction of the world of being: intermediary period of nihilism: before there is yet present the strength to reverse values and to deify becoming and the apparent world as the only world, and to call them good. B. Nihilism as a normal phenomenon can be a symptom of increasing strength or of increasing weakness: partly, because the strength to create, to will, has so increased that it no longer requires these total interpretations and introductions of meaning ('present tasks', the state, etc.); partly, because even the creative strength to create meaning has declined and disappointment becomes the dominant condition. The incapability of believing in a 'meaning', 'unbelief.' [WP 585]

> Nihilism as a normal condition. It can be a sign of strength: the spirit may have grown so strong that previous goals ('convictions', articles of faith) have become incommensurate (for a faith generally expresses the constraint of conditions of existence, submission to the authority of circumstances under which one flourishes, grows, gains power). Or a sign of the lack of strength to posit for oneself, productively, a goal, a why, a faith. It reaches its maximum of relative strength as a violent force of destruction—as active nihilism ...
>
> Nihilism ... as a sign of weakness. The strength of the spirit may be worn out, exhausted, so that previous goals and values have become incommensurate and no longer are believed; so that the synthesis of values and goals (on which every strong culture rests) dissolves and the individual values war against each other: disintegration—and whatever refreshes, heals, calms, numbs, emerges into the foreground in various disguises, religious or moral, or political, or aesthetic, etc." [WP 23]
>
> Nihilism. It is ambiguous:
>
> A. Nihilism as a sign of increased power of the spirit: as active nihilism.
>
> B. Nihilism as decline and recession of the power of the spirit: as passive nihilism. [WP 22]

What can we infer from these three aphorisms? Firstly, we get to know that there is a nihilism which arises out of strength which Nietzsche calls active nihilism, and a nihilism which arises out of weakness which he calls passive nihilism. Secondly, we are told that nihilism is only dominant in an intermediary period, in between periods with absolute standards, i.e. epistemological, metaphysical, ethical, or aesthetic criteria. It is not said that this applies only to the global political level, but it can also be essential for an understanding of the personal ethical development, as I will show later.

How do these points apply to our discussion? Since nihilism is only dominant in an intermediary period, in between periods with absolute standards, it tells us that we need three different stages of progression. Absolute standards can be applied or taken with respect to epistemological, metaphysical, ethical and aesthetic criteria, as well as any combination of any of these domains. It can also apply on a personal, as well as on a global level. This means that we can talk about the development from a protected spoiled child to an heroic adult, as well as the change from a Buddhist to a Capitalistic materialistic society, or a

Christian to a Scientific one, if we want to reveal the possibilites of use of this notion. One cannot generalise about whether a development involving the intermediary state of nihilism is an improvement or an impoverishment of a society, for it can be both. So one does not have to give a peculiar judgement about nihilism—it is not an object of praise or blame per se. It depends upon whether it is active or passive nihilism, i.e. whether it enhances or impoverishes the life of the group or the individual in question. Let me give some examples for active and passive nihilism. I will explain the problem in question through the example of an individual human being who is a power-constellation constituted by many individual power-quanta. In the next main part I will apply this principle to societies, for this is what Nietzsche does.

In the first example I will deal with passive nihilism. Imagine a boy, twelve years of age, who is an excellent football player. He wants to become an professional, and everyone supports and expects him to become one—especially his father. His *Ueber-Ich* demands that he becomes a professional football player; this *Ueber-Ich* is the set of absolute standards. Yet, it happens that the boy has a car accident and loses a leg. It is impossible for him to fulfil his aim anymore. His actual strength does not enable him to do what he wanted to do anymore. He is too weak for the aims he set himself, so he has to give up this aim. This brings him into a period of passive nihilism. He does not know what to do with his life, because he lost his old aim. For some time he loses his sense in life, there is no more structure to which he can stick. Suddenly he realises that he is quite a good writer, and he writes a novel. It gets published and sells well. In this way he has found a new absolute standard to which he can dedicate himself, and which appeals to his actual power potential. Due to his finding or creating such a new aim (erecting an *Ideal-Ich* which demand lower aims of him than the ones he initially aimed for. The boy still regards a professional football player to be more powerful than a novelist), he manages to transcend the intermediary period of nihilism. The actual development of course is much more complicated, but this schematic progression should have made clear the concept of passive nihilism.

In the next example I will be concerned with active nihilism. Imagine a tall, slim, very beautiful, poor girl, thirteen years old. She is not very educated and not very clever either. Everybody expects her to become a waitress or something comparable. Her *Ueber-Ich* just expects her to get a normal job, marry someone as soon as possible, and have some children. This is the initial set of absolute standards. However, at Victoria tube station a man approaches her, tells her that he wants her to become a model, gives her his card, and leaves. She is very flattered, and straight away gives up all her old aims. She wants to become a model, and yet, she is not sure, whether the man was serious, or whether he has rather dubious intentions. This uncertainty leaves her in a state of insecurity. She has abandoned her old aims, but is not yet sure whether the new ones are realistic for her. Yet, she abandoned the old ones out of strength, because her actual abilities are higher than what the old aims demanded for her. So this nihilism came about out of strength, it is active nihilism. A couple of weeks later, after she has found out that the model agency in question is a genuine one, she phones the company, goes to them, and gets employed. She integrates her aim to be a model within her *Ideal-Ich*, and thereby has managed to transcend nihilism and build up a new absolute standard for herself which is higher than her prior aims. Of course the actual development here is far more complicated as well. This schema should have provided with an initial understanding of active nihilism.

As one can see through these two examples, one can find nihilism in many different disguises. In Freud it turns up under the heading of narcissism. According to Freud we evaluate our actions on the basis of our *Ueber-Ich* until we are satisfied with its demands. The *Ueber-Ich* is constituted out of the morals of our parents and teachers *et cetera*, yet, it is not likely that its demands correspond to our actual ones. Therefore there will be a time, usually during our teenage years, when we become so dissatisfied with our aims that we start to abandon them. Then a period of personal nihilism begins. At some stage we try to create a new *Ideal-Ich* according to our own demands which, if done well, does correspond to our actual potential. From then on we strive to reach our *Ideal-Ich*. This stage of personal orientation is referred to as narcissism by Freud. So narcissism is an essential part of our development, and it does not have to be unhealthy. Only if the goals we have set for ourselves are too high and we do not give them up but strive unrealistically towards them, then we can get caught in an unhealthy form of narcissism. Once we reach our *Ideal-Ich*, the period of nihilism is over, and we can live according to our new set of values.

Another way to describe a period of nihilism in an individual human life can be found in C. G. Jung—though Nietzsche does not only apply it at that personal level, but also at a political global level. The phenomena in question is the same as in Freud, but in Jung's case it takes on a more complex form. Jung divides a human life into four essential phases[31]. After birth we enter the childhood phase, then early maturity, middle age, and finally late maturity which is ended by our death. In between these phases we find transitory phases: there is the adolescent transition, mid-life transition, and late life transition. In each of these transitory phases, we have to revaluate our values; we have to abandon our old aims, for they no longer apply to our demands and needs, and have to find new ones better suited for our potentials, needs and demands. The Archetypal programme for the adolescent transgression reveals that this theory refers to the same phenomena Freud explained before. Anthony Stevens in his book "On Jung" describes the developmentary processes of this phase as follows: "if one is to leave home, support oneself in the world, attract (and keep) a sexual partner and eventually start a family of one's own, then the bonds of the parents must be loosened, a job prepared for and found, sexual development completed, an appropriate persona acquired and enough confidence and self-esteem achieved to be able to hold one's head up in society." [Stevens (1990): P. 117)]. Yet in the process of this development one has to face nihilism, because the new absolute standards are yet uncertain and the old ones already abandoned.

Let me repeat that nihilism out of strength is what Nietzsche refers to as active nihilism and the nihilism out of weakness is passive nihilism. To understand why he uses the terms active and passive we have to reconsider his metaphysics. Given Nietzsche's metaphysics the whole world is will to power with a limited amount of power-quanta—some exist on their own, others in power-constellations. The highest feeling of power a power-constellation can achieve is if it has managed to interpret the world in such a way that the world of Becoming is seen as a world of Being. This can only be done by one's spirit. While a power-constellation is working on such an interpretation, it has to have the strongest will to power. All power quanta, and power-constellations permanently strive for an increase of their own power.

Given this background one can understand that an increase of power is related to activity, while a decrease is linked with passivity. We all aim for power, because we are will to power, and only the power-constellations which manage to increase their power are the ones who fulfil their

31 Compare Sorgner (2001b) P. 249-254.

drive actively. If a power-constellation does not increase its power, then this cannot have happened due to the activity of the power-constellation itself, but had to be caused by the influence of other power-constellations. Because the power-constellation was passive with respect to that development, we can now understand where the terminology of active and passive comes from.

After dealing with the vague rationality of progression, we can go a bit deeper into the actual process of change, for Nietzsche says more about it than I have mentioned so far. A process of change starts from absolute standards, moves into nihilism, and ends up with absolute standards again. How can one see that the original set of absolute standards is about to fade away? What are the symptoms of decay?

> Consequences of decadence ...pessimism" [WP 42]
>
> Pessimism as a prelimary form of nihilism" [WP 9]
>
> Concept of decadence.—Waste, decay, elimination, need not be condemned: they are necessary consequences of life, of the growth of life ... A society is not free to remain young." [WP 40]
>
> On the concept of decadence.
>
> 1. Skepticism is a consequence of decadence, as is libertinism of the spirit.
>
> 2. The corruption of morals is a consequence of decadence (weakness of the will, need for strong stimuli). ...
>
> 4. Nihilism is no cause but merely the logical result of decadence.
>
> ... so pleasure and displeasure become foreground problems." [WP 43]

These four aphorisms tell us a lot about the actual progression of change, and how it can be that the set of absolute standards to which an individual or a society adheres can alter. As Nietzsche says it is a necessity of the dynamics of life that nothing remains young and that decay has to come about for everything. This decay is called decadence, and decadence arises when active as well as when passive nihilism comes about. So decadence is not necessarily something that has to be rejected. Decadence arises whenever the actual strength of the body (individual, society ...) in question no longer corresponds to its own absolute principles, i.e. what demands are placed on it. It can be that the body is too strong for his own principles as well as that it is too weak.

The last aphorism states that decadence effects a liberation of the spirit. We should briefly remember which function Nietzsche attributed to spirit. According to Nietzsche, the highest form of power is achieved if spirit imposes Being on Becoming, interprets the world so that one sees it as unchanging, although in fact it is permanently changing. This is the highest form of power, and it can only be brought about by spirit. Given that the whole world is will to power for Nietzsche, one should be aware of the importance of spirit now. We all are will to power and therefore want to gain as much power as possible. Spirit can enable us to gain the highest form of power at the moment, by interpreting the world of change as a world of stability. It can do so by imposing structures, forms and order or certain categories on Becoming, and in this way spirit develops specific forms and becomes more and more powerful. Yet, if we say the spirit gets liberated with the beginning of decadence, then this means that all the forms which were developed dissolve and vanish. Since the forms of the spirit are categories which enable us to have a stable picture of the world, categories which help us to interpret the world, and senses and values according to which we can act and judge[32], all our knowledge which is built out of these categories vanishes and leave us in a senseless, purposeless, valueless, alien world. This is exactly the point Nietzsche makes in the aphorisms in question.

All our habits get corrupted in an age of decadence. This is a consequence of the vanishing of the forms of our spirit. Nihilism is not the cause but the logic of decadence, and this means that nihilism was not there before decadence and brought it about, but that nihilism and decadence are necessarily inter-linked. The forms of the spirit start to vanish and with that nihilism begins, that is, the world loses its sense, purpose, order and values for us. Due to these developments pain and pleasure become our primary problems, as Nietzsche points out. This is also apparent in Nietzsche's remark that pessimism follows from decadence, and that pessimism is closely linked to nihilism. Pessimism is the view that in every life the pain outweighs the pleasure experienced. Given Nietzsche's metaphysics it becomes obvious why pessimism and pain and pleasure as our primary problems arise, because once all the forms, principles, senses, values are gone, all that we are left with are our experiences of pain and pleasure, and as one can see at the respective

32 When spirit is creating forms, it is simply filling in content into the different branches of philosophy, as mentioned in D, e.g. epistemology, metaphysics, ethics.

discussion (in main part one) pain always has to outweigh pleasure, e.g. that pessimism has to follow, once we estimate everything on the basis of pain and pleasure. The fact that pain and pleasure become our primary problems, because they are everything on which we are basing an judgement for our actions, is called psychological hedonism. Out of this pessimism is bound to arise, according to Nietzsche. One can take various attitudes towards this pessimism—one can either accept it and try to minimise both pleasure and pain (main aim avoid pain, yet with this pleasure vanishes as well), or one can rebel against it by attempting to aim for as much pleasure as possible, even though this causes one a lot of pain as well which is called hedonism in the next aphorism. Of course it could also be the case that one can come across a combination out of these two reactions:

> the 'predominance of suffering over pleasure' or the opposite (hedonism): these two doctrines are already signposts to nihilism. For in both of these cases no ultimate meaning is posited except the appearance of pleasure and displeasure. But that is how a kind of man speaks that no longer dares to posit a will, a purpose, a meaning: for any healthier kind of man the value of life is certainly not measured by the standard of these trifles. And suffering might predominate, and in spite of that a powerful will might exist, a Yes to life, a need for this predominance. [WP 35]

This aphorism clearly explains the difference between nihilistic periods, and periods with absolute standards. In nihilistic times all actions are judged on the basis of pain and pleasure, whereas in times with absolute standards one simply sticks to one's absolute standards irrespective of the pain and pleasure accompanied by them. This seems to go against all our intuitions. One usually believes that one justifies one's actions by reference to pain and pleasure. If one is asked, why one is not doing some action X (washing up, tidying up ...), then one usually replies that one does not like, enjoy it, e.g. it makes us experience pain. If one is asked, why some other action Z (eating chocolate cake ...) is one's hobby, one usually replies that one enjoys it, one has a good time whenever one is doing it, e.g. it is pleasurable. Nietzsche, however, reveals to us that all these sort of replies show that we are living in decadent times, in a period of the resurgence of nihilism. He thinks that life can even be worth living if we permanently have to suffer, because according to him a healthy individual does not evaluate actions on the basis of pain and pleasure, but on the basis of a system of self imposed values. This, however, can only be the case, if one has created strict forms within one's spirit which provide oneself with senses, values *et cetera*. This is a point which one cannot stress often enough. This does not mean that in sticking to absolute principles one has to suffer permanently, rather that it does not matter whether one suffers or experiences pleasure, as long as one acts in accord with one's principles or values..

At this stage the development from psychological states with absolute standards to nihilism should be clear. It progresses from an age of absolute standards, to decadence, pessimism and nihilism—no matter whether it is active or passive nihilism. Yet, Nietzsche distinguishes between classic and romantic pessimism; classic pessimism brings about active nihilism, and romantic pessimism passive nihilism [KSA vol. 13, 14 (25)]. Nietzsche identifies the present times with nihilistic times. He was not the only one to see it that way, as one can imagine given the variety of thinkers who employed the notion of "nihilism." As I said before, the problem of nihilism in relation to our present times is more often discussed in continental philosophy, and continental writers in general, than it is in Anglo-American philosophy. It might be helpful to consider some of the others cultural innovators for whom the problem of nihilism was extremely relevant. Nietzsche himself referred to some of them in his work: Tolstoy and Wagner, belong to the artistic decadence [AC 7]. This does not have to be construed as a dismissal of them, as I have explained before. However, he objects against all forms of romantic pessimism which arise according to him in the following thinkers and movements:

> The pessimism of Schopenhauer for example, and so for Alfred de Vigny's, Dostoevsky's, Leopardi's, Pascal's—the pessimism of all great nihilistic religions (Brahminism, Buddhism, Christianity; they may all be termed 'nihilistic', because they have all glorified the concept opposed to life—Nothing—as their goal, as their highest good, as 'God') [KSA 13, 14 (25), PF]

I will deal with the nihilistic religions later on. Here I just wish to stress that even in the case of the thinkers he has objections against, he can have a high respect for them as well, as one can see in the case of Dostoevsky:

> Dostoevsky, the only psychologist, incidentally, from whom I had something to learn; he ranks among the most beautiful strokes of fortune in my life, even more than my discovery of Stendhal. This

> profound human being who was ten times right in his low estimate of the Germans, lived for a long time among the convicts of Siberia—hardened criminals for whom there was no way back to society—and found them very different from what he himself had expected: they were carved out of just about the best, hardest, and most valuable wood that grows anywhere on Russian soil."= [TI "Skirmishes of an Untimely Man" 45]

He could not have praised Dostoevsky any more highly. He clearly regarded him even more highly than Stendhal, of whose formula "the only excuse for God is that he does not exist," Nietzsche was overtly envious, according to Camus [Camus (1962): P. 58] Nietzsche had not only read Dostoevsky, but also other Russian nihilistic novelists like Turgenev. Let me briefly reflect upon some aspects of their nihilism.

Firstly I wish to mention Turgenev's novel "Fathers and Sons" in which the main character Bazaros is called a nihilist. A nihilst is a person who is defined as someone "who recognises nothing" by Nikoplai Petrovich, but also as someone who "looks at everything critically" according to Arkady [Turgenev (1965): P. 94]. In Bazarov's case the notion implies that he rejects the importance of art and religion, but he himself says "I do not believe in anything: and what is science—science in the abstract? There are sciences, as there are trades and professions, but abstract science just does not exist." [Turgenev (1965): P. 98] This however seems to me to be not a proper form of nihilism, because he does acknowledge the truth of the particular sciences, although he claims not to believe in anything anymore. A nihilist, according to the former analysis, could not do this.

Yet, there are other novelists who come closer to Nietzsche's analysis of nihilism, e.g. Lermontov and Oscar Wilde. Both these novelists aim at an exploration of hedonism, yet I do not think that they agree with Nietzsche that pessimism is necessarily linked with psychological hedonism, i.e. the view that we judge all our actions on the basis of pain and pleasure. Lermontov's hedonism especially becomes obvious in his chapter "Princess Mary" in his "A Hero of our Times" [Lermontov (1966): P. 91-174], where Lermontov's hero, Perochin, is playing around with the feelings of young Princess Mary: "I shall enjoy myself. Enjoy myself! I've passed that stage in life when all one seeks is happiness and when the heart feels the need to love someone with passion and intensity" [Lermontov (1966): P. 111]. In Oscar Wilde hedonism is best expressed in the second chapter of his master work "The Picture of Dorian Gray" [Wilde (1974)]. Here Lord Henry, one of the main characters of the work, explains the concept of "A new Hedonism" [Wilde (1974): P. 22] which implies that "The only way to get rid of a temptation is to yield to it." [Wilde (1974): P. 18] However, there are other thinkers who come even closer to Nietzsche's understanding of nihilism, namely the ones who take pessimism as a basis for their estimation of the world. In that respect, Schopenhauer, Camus, and Dostoevsky have to be mentioned.

Due to Camus's pessimism, for him the question whether to commit suicide or not was the only philosophical question. His answer to this question was not to seek as much pleasure as possible, as the previous thinkers did, and also not to avoid pain. He accepted that he would have to experience more pain than pleasure, but was giving himself new values which are implicit in his formulation of the Myth of Sisyphus—in this way he belongs among Nietzsche's philosophers of the Future, the creators of new values. Camus' new values are explicitly stated in his chapter "Quality instead of quantity" [Camus (1956): P. 54-57]. There he states his goal in life: it is not to live as well as possible, but to live as long as possible. This is a suggestion worth considering, for it clearly rejects the option of suicide. By putting forward new values, he has done the same as Nietzsche did, or as Dostoevsky, whom we shall consider next.

"Dostoevsky knew nothing about Nietzsche or his work. On the other hand, Nietzsche read Dostoevsky and was enamored by of his writings. He read 'Notes from the House of the Dead', a garbled version of 'Notes from the Underground', 'The Devils', and probably 'The Idiot.' It appears that he did not read 'Crime and Punishment' or 'The Brothers Karamasov'.. Nietzsche certainly found in Dostoevsky rich material confirming his notion of the crisis of nihilism ... Nietzsche sought a 'countermovement' in the creation of new values, in a philosophical outlook that would accept the world as it is ... Dostoevsky, on the other hand, turned to traditional Christian values for a solution to the problem of nihilism." [Jackson (1993): P. 20-21]. However, Dostoevsky's solution to nihilism seems to me rather to have been a choice due to his temperament, than to his actual conviction. Dostoevsky himself said in a letter to N. D. Fonvizina [Jackson (1993): P. 246]: "if somebody proved to me that Christ was outside the truth, and it really were so that the truth was outside of Christ, then I would rather remain with Christ than with the truth." It is interesting to note that for Dostoevsky Christianity and love of humanity is necessarily linked to the belief in the immortality of the soul (in "Diary of a Writer" December 1976 issue [Jackson (1993) P. 294]): "I declare (once again for the time being) without proof that love for humanity is even quite unthinkable, incomprehensible and quite impossible without concurrent faith in the immortality of the human soul." Whatever the reasons for Dostoevsky to put forward his solution to nihilism—and I will not go into any further detail here—, let us consider his attitude towards the world first. I think that his attitude is represented very well in what Ivan in "The Brothers Karamasov" is referring to when he talks about the suffering of all the innocent children. Yet, it comes out in his other works as well, for example the prisoners in the "Notes from the House of the Dead" or Liza and the Underground man in his "Notes from the Underground." It then becomes obvious that Dostoevsky's analysis of the world is pessimistic, and given Jackson's analysis of Dostoevsky's work it becomes obvious that Nietzsche was far from alone in his understanding of the world. Nietzsche and Dostoevsky—two men with great self awareness (and my two favourite thinkers and writers)—agree in their basic outlook on the world, although in their reaction to this world view they differed.

Nietzsche describes how different types of human beings become affected by pessimism and its accompaniment nihilism.

> The development from pessimism into nihilism .... one discovers of what material one has built the 'true world': and now all one has left is the repudiated world, and one adds this supreme disappointment to the reasons why it deserves to be repudiated. At this point nihilism is reached: all that one has left are the values that pass judgement—nothing else. Here the problem of strength and weakness originates:
> 1. the weak perish of it;
> 2. those who are stronger destroy what does not perish;
> 3. those who are strongest overcome the values that pass judgement.
> In sum this constitutes the tragic age. [WP 37]

As mentioned before, Nietzsche believes that pessimism is a consequence of decadence. Once pessimism becomes accepted among the members of a society or by any individual, this view has various effects on the different types of individuals. For this purpose he divides human beings into the weak, the stronger, and the strongest in spirit. If the weak estimate life solely on the basis of pain and pleasure, then this will destroy them fairly soon, because they are not in a position to gain much and intense pleasure and avoid the pain. They are sickly, often ill, with lesser capacities, and do not have the appropriate means to get many kicks, high jinx, and pleasure. That is the reason why they only ever get little pleasure, but have to endure a lot of pain. The stronger ones keep on destroying the principles, values, believes, senses, and also the weaker people that have not been destroyed yet, because this provides them with a way to gain some pleasure and with this some sort of justification for their life. For as one can infer from the section on pain and pleasure (in main part one), it is painful to create new forms, but pleasurable to get rid of them. This sort of justification is a typical option for individuals in decadent times. At least these men have got some means to gain pleasure and can therefore relate to the spirit of the times which is formless—with respect to absolute principles. Only the strongest can overcome nihilism by creating new values, senses, truths et cetera. This corresponds to what I have mentioned already in main part one, where I discussed what the highest form of power is. One has gained the highest form of power, and belongs therefore to the strongest if one has managed to impose Being on Becoming, put forward an interpretation of the world which makes the world of change appear as a stable world, impose forms and order onto the existential flux. Some of these forms stand for values and senses—others for positions on other philosophical issues. Senses are values and vice versa; they are absolute principles on which one can base ones actions, and they are independent of pain and pleasure. It is not the case that if one judges every action on the basis of pain and pleasure only (psychological hedonism), one has already created new values, because new values, senses, and standards become absolute when they are independent of pain and pleasure. Senses and values are types of action grouped together in a consistent fashion, however this consistency which is a necessary constituent of absolute standards, and principles, is not given, if one acts on the basis of pain and pleasure only—for what can give us pleasure in one situation can cause us pain in another one (a bar of chocolate, after one has not eaten anything for 3 days & a bar of chocolates, after one has had ten bars already). This should make it clear that if one takes pain and pleasure as a basis for the estimation of our actions, then one cannot have a consistent set of types of action which is an essential precondition for times with absolute principles.

2.2.2 Schopenhauer's Nihilism & Plato's Nihilism

I have already explained that Nietzsche, Dostoevsky and Camus created new values to escape from nihilism. I have also explained that Lermontov and Wilde also judged everything on the basis of pain and pleasure (without necessarily having a pessimistic outlook onto the world), but that they simply tried to maximise their pleasure, e.g. they did not create new values. The other option mentioned which one can take, if one judges everything on the basis of pain and pleasure, is to avoid pain (and together with this one also cannot get any pleasure, as it will turn out). This option was turned into a religion—namely Buddhism. One could refer to Buddhism also as Buddhist nihilism or Schopenhauer's nihilism [WP 17], because Nietzsche takes them to be identical. Of course, there are many different kinds of Buddhism, and not all of them correspond to the concept Nietzsche attributed to them, but I think that there are enough reasons for holding that this is a sensible way of expression.

> I hope that my condemnation of Christianity has not involved me in any injustice to a related religion with an even larger number of adherents: Buddhism. Both belong together as nihilistic religions—they are religions of decadence—but they differ most remarkably .... Buddhism ... does no longer say 'struggle against sin', but, duly respectful of reality, 'struggle against suffering.' [AC 20]
>
> The two great nihilistic movements: (a) Buddhism, (b) Christianity ... The latter has only now attained to approximately the state of culture in which it can fulfil its original vocation—a level to which it belongs—in which it can show itself pure. [WP 220]
>
> The exhausted want rest, relaxation, peace, calm—the happiness of the nihilistic religions and philosophies; the rich and living want victory, opponents overcome, the overflow of the feeling of power across wider domains than hithero. All healthy functions of the organism have this need—and the whole organism is such a complex of systems struggling for an increase of the feeling of power. [WP 703]
>
> Buddha against the 'Crucified.' Among the nihilistic religions, one may already clearly distinguish the Christian from the Buddhist. The

> Buddhist religion is the expression of a fine evening ... [it] is lacking: bitterness ... a lofty spiritual love ...even from these it is resting. The Christian movement is a degeneracy movement composed of reject and refuse elements of every kind: it is not the expression of the decline of a race, it is from the first an agglomeration of forms of morbidity crowding together and seeking one another out— ... it takes the side of idiots and utters a curse on the spirit. Rancor against the gifted, learned, spiritually independent: it detects in them the well-constituted, the masterful. [WP 154]

Buddhism fights against suffering, which already implies that Buddhists also have a fundamentally pessimistic conception of the world, this means that they think that the body has to go through more pain than pleasure. Their solution to this problem is to aim for the avoidance of pain, and grant that with this aim they also have to accept the loss of any form of pleasure. That is the reason why Nietzsche regards Buddhism as a nihilistic religion, whose happiness lies in calmness and peace. Given Nietzsche's own understanding of the world as will to power this opinion of course also expresses something about adherents to that religion. If the adherents of such a religion do not stick to their natural drive anymore, then this shows that they regard themselves as too weak to aim for great goals, and therefore take the best possible option open to them—the avoidance of pain and pleasure. Buddhism is referred to as nihilistic religion because it presupposes pessimism. Its reaction to pessimism is to search for happiness in a state beyond pain and pleasure (*pari-nirvana*).

One can also refer to Buddhist nihilism as Schopenhauer's nihilism, because of the similarity between these two world views. Schopenhauer's metaphysics focuses on will to life and this leads him to pessimism. Due to the permanent striving of the will which causes us pain it is impossible to achieve a permanent state of personal satisfaction. He himself says: "All willing springs from lack, from deficiency, and thus from suffering. Fulfilment brings this to an end; yet for one wish that is fulfilled there remain at least ten that are denied. Further, desiring lasts a long time, demands and requests go on to infinity; fulfilment is short and meted out sparingly. But even the final satisfaction is only apparent; the wish fulfilled at once makes way for a new one, the former is a known delusion, the latter a delusion not as yet known. No attained object of willing can give a satisfaction that lasts and no longer declines." [quoted in Budd (1992): P. 84-85]. There are only two ways according to Schopenhauer to escape from this suffering. One option is through aesthetic contemplation; but this is only a short term solution. The second and more lasting option is via asceticism; this involves "chastity, fasting, and a general denial of the body's needs" [Hamlyn (1980): P. 148], and also "a renunciation of one's true nature and therefore a denial of the will itself." [Hamlyn (1980): P. 148]. For if there is no more willing, then there is no more suffering either. This brief description should make clearer the similarity between Buddhism and Schopenhauer's philosophy, and it should also lend support to Nietzsche's claim that this is a form of nihilism. Due to the relation of Buddhism with pessimism, Nietzsche, according to his own scheme, is also justified in regarding Buddhism as being linked to a decadent race.

As revealed in the foregoing aphorisms Nietzsche not only calls Buddhism but also Christianity a nihilistic religion. Christianity can also be thought of as Plato's nihilism, because, according to Nietzsche: "for Christianity is Platonism for 'the people'" [BGE preface]

Christianity does not represent the decadence of a race, as Buddhism does. What is decadent about Christianity is that it only appeals to the weak, the sick, the stupid, and attacks the strong, the talented, and the strong in spirit, according to Nietzsche. It appeals to them because Christianity regards this world as a test of God: One has to act in accord with what is good (charity, humility) and avoid doing what is evil (being strong, powerful), so that one has a chance to pass the test. If one passes it, one will have a blissful after-life which is the only true life, the only worth while life, because this is where one remains for all eternity. If one does not pass the test, then one has to suffer in one's afterlife (at least for a certain period of time). This is an interpretation of Christianity in the spirit of Nietzsche; more complete exegesis of Nietzsche's thought on Christian doctrine is not needed for our purposes. According to him, Christianity claims that the sick, the suffering, the good will have a blissful afterlife, and the strong, the healthy, and the powerful will not. Therefore it is understandable that the weak the sick, the suffering are the one to whom this religion appeals, for these people are being promised a blissful afterlife. What is nihilistic about this religion is not that Christians are weak people, but that this religion posits a goal which is, according to Nietzsche, non existent. The good believers are being promised an after-world which will never be reached, because for Nietzsche there is no such thing as an after-world. The meaning of the notion of "nihilism" with respect to Christianity is quite different than the one used before, because in the case of the aforementioned it was always related to the loss of strict rules and morals, the arrival of pain and pleasure as the basis for the estimation of one's actions, and pessimism. These criteria do not seem to apply to what is "nihilistic" about Christianity. Christianity which is related rather to the opposite of these two principles, as Nietzsche himself points out.

> What were the advantages of the Christian moral hypothesis?
> 1. It granted man an absolute value, as opposed to his smallness and accidental occurence in the flux of becoming and passing away;
> 2. It served the advocates of God insofar as it conceded to the world, in spite of suffering and evil, the character of perfection—including 'freedom': evil appeared full of meaning.
> 3. It posited that man had a knowledge of absolute values and thus adequate knowledge precisely regarding what is most important.
> 4. It prevented man from despising himself as man, from taking sides against life; from despairing of knowledge: it was a means of preservation.
> In sum: morality was the great antidote against practical and theoretical nihilism. [WP 4]

Here one can see that Nietzsche does recognize the strengths of Christianity and that it is not related to nihilism in the previously mentioned sense of the word but that this sort of nihilism which I called Plato's nihilism[33] has a different sense, e.g. Christianity is nihilistic in the sense that it sets aims which cannot be achieved, which are non existent, according to Nietzsche's metaphysics. Nietzsche's metaphysics includes the claim that will can only act upon will and therefore the possibility that a separate world can be achieved is excluded on a priori grounds.

This shows that it is not quite appropriate that Nietzsche used the expression "nihilistic religion" for Christianity as well as Buddhism, because by doing this, he seems to imply that the concept of "nihilism" remains the same no matter which religion he is talking about. This, however, is clearly not the case; with respect to Buddhism "nihilism" has the same meaning as "nihilism" usually has in Nietzsche. Yet, whenever it is claimed that Christianity is a "nihilistic religion," then the sense of "nihilism" is a completely different one, i.e. related to an unreachable goal or a separate world or a nothing, whose linguistic existence is based

33 Christianity is Platonism for the masses, according to Nietzsche [BGE preface].

on the human ability to invent. So Nietzsche's use of language here is misleading and inappropriate, because the notion of "nihilistic religion" is ambiguous without Nietzsche making it obvious that this is the case.

However, the distinction between Plato's nihilism and Schopenhauer's nihilism was not my main concern in this section, rather nihilism—active and passive—and its role in history.

There is another philosopher, whose main concern is the attitude one should take with respect to contemporary nihilism—Peter Sloterdijk. In his main work "The Critique of Cynical Reason" [Sloterdijk (1983)], he criticises contemporary cynicism which, according to Sloterdijk, is enlightened false consciousness. As a suitable alternative he puts forward kynicism which is enlightened correct consciousness although he does not express it in these terms. What these attitudes have in common is that both of them are held by people with an enlightened consciousness. Someone has to accept all the destructive critiques which have taken place during the enlightenment to have an enlightened consciousness. These critiques destroyed the belief in Christianity, and the possibility of knowledge and absolute values, to put it briefly. So for someone to have an enlightened consciousness is just another way to refer to a nihilist. Both the cynic as well as the kynic are nihilists. However, the consciousness of the cynic is false, because he is miserable due to nihilism or the loss of all his beliefs. A kynic, on the other hand, is cheeky, life-affirming, and joyful. A kynic affirms the whole body and does not let himself be restricted by old outgrown habits. Sloterdijk wants us to realise that we do not have to be cynics, but it would be better for us to be kynics.

This analysis of his world view seems to imply that he is not a pessimist. Yet the characterisations of these two types, and the description of enlightened consciousness make it clear that he also estimates one's actions on the basis of pleasure and pain alone. Sloterdijk's very refreshing treatment of the problem of nihilism shows that the problem which was pointed out by Nietzsche more than a hundred years ago is still a problem which has to be tackled. Sloterdijk's solution also includes an awareness of the failure of the two significant immanent solutions to nihilism which were put into practice in this century—Fascism and Communism—two post-Christian political systems. Therefore he does not put forward another system of grand values but simply aims to alter one's attitude towards the experiences one has. I think this is an alternative theory worth considering in this book, and also worth bearing in mind personally.

With this section I have completed the second main part which is entitled Dionysos. What I have to do now, is to take main part one and two and show that they are not inconsistent. We have already had to realise the importance of consistency within Nietzsche's philosophy when I talked about the role of the intellect in Nietzsche. However, main part one and two appear as inconsistent. On the one hand, there is no truth, on the other hand the world is will to power and eternally recurring. On the one hand, there are no absolute universal values, on the other hand we all aim for power, and human beings are dissimilar with respect to value. I will show in the next section that all of these contradictions are only apparent contradictions, that is, that they all are reconciled in Nietzsche's philosophy.

Apollo & Dionysos Reconciled

3.

In this chapter I will finally put forward a solution to the problem I intend to solve with this work. As the title of my book suggests, I am concerned with the relation of Nietzsche's metaphysical claims with his remarks about truth. This relation has been a matter of great controversy, many commentators have regarded Nietzsche as an irrational thinker due to his apparently inconsistent claims with respect to these two issues. An irrational thinker is one who holds contradictory positions (p and not-p), i.e. who is inconsistent. Yet, as the subtitle implies, I wish to show that Nietzsche is not inconsistent, and that it is important for him not to be so. This claim, however, seems to go against my analysis so far, because it might appear as if the Nietzsche of the Apollo section and the Nietzsche of the Dionysos section defend mutually inconsistent positions. This section will show that no such inconsistency exists. Firstly, I will briefly point out the apparent inconsistencies, then I put forward my solution to this problem. When I deal with my interpretation of Nietzsche's solution, I will refer to Nietzsche's philosophy of history. Only if we take this into consideration, can we understand why Nietzsche's views on metaphysics and truth do not clash. A substantial part of my account of Nietzsche's views on the progression of history will concern how Nietzsche saw his own position within this progression. These reflections on Nietzsche's philosophy of history are also of immense relevance for the understanding of our contemporary culture, our attitude towards values, post-modernism, the sickness of our times, the increasing importance of Pop-culture, the Communist and Fascist world views and reflections about our future.

3.1.

3.1.1 The Problem (in detail) On the Apparent Inconsistencies of Nietzsche's Thought

Firstly, I wish to give some examples of major interpretations of Nietzsche regarding the question of consistency in his philosophy. On this matter, I will show how they interpreted the relation between his views on truth and his metaphysical claims. One of the clearest expositions of the problem is to be found in Danto:

> In these last pages I wish only to raise once again the obvious question regarding the status of Nietzsche's philosophy in terms of its own conception of philosophical activity. Was his philosophy, too, a matter of mere convention, fiction, and Will-to-power? To put it sophomorically but no less vexingly, was it his intention, in saying that nothing is true, to say something true? If he succeeded, then of course he failed, for if it is true that nothing is true, something is true after all. If it is false, then something again is true. If, again, what he says is as arbitrary as he has said, critically, that all of philosophy is, why should we accept him if we are to reject the others? And if not arbitrary, how can it be right? How can what he says be true if he has said what the truth is? Nietzsche was alive to these difficulties, I believe. As he wrote in Beyond Good and Evil: 'Supposing that this, too, is only an interpretation—and one will be eager enough to raise this objection. Well—so much the better.' I suppose that we are to judge him by the criterion we have in fact always employed, our philosophical ideologies notwithstanding: by whether his philosophy works in life. He might continue: If you do not care for the forms I give to things, you give things your own. Philosophy is a creative business, and the way is always open. Philosophy is a contest of will with will. Insofar as you oppose my philosophy, you illustrate and confirm it.
>
> I doubt that everyone would be satisfied with such an answer, for I am not even certain that it is an answer. But I have no other to offer. [Danto (1965): P. 230]

I am not satisfied with Danto's answer, for I think it over-simplifies the issue and I think that I have a more complete one to offer. Although, I must admit that his basic way of thinking takes a similar direction as mine. However, the way he expresses it, and justifies it, is far too narrow, limited and incomplete. A similar response was given by Nehamas. He points out:

> Perspectivism does not result in the relativism that holds that any view is as good as any other; it holds that one's own views are the best for oneself without implying that they need be good for anyone else. [Nehamas (1985): P. 72]

> Having presented his perspectivism not so much as a traditional theory of knowledge but as the view that all efforts to know are also efforts of particular people to live particular kinds of lives for particular reasons, he now applies that view to itself. [Nehamas (1985): P. 73]

However, these sort of replies seem to me to be inadequate, because they do not seriously take into consideration Nietzsche's metaphysics of the will to power and the eternal recurrence. On the one hand one could say that they do by claiming that Nietzsche's metaphysics was what he needed to live the sort of life he wanted to live, or that was good for him. Yet, in this case Nietzsche's philosophy does not say anything about the basis on which people decide what sort of life is best for them, because then his metaphysics would only be the one good for himself. It seems as if Nehamas' reply ends up in some sort of relativism for Nietzsche, although Nehamas claims that it does not, because he says that everyone is choosing the best life for oneself. I think that this is indeed a relativistic position, because he does not say what a good life consists in. Nehamas might reply to this that people simply have a conception of a good life, or that they develop it creatively. However, this again is not an adequate reply to the accusation of relativism, because he cannot articulate the conditions under which each individual conception of a good life arises, or on what basis we create our concept of a good life. Therefore we have to conclude that Nehamas' interpretation of Nietzsche's perspectivism does indeed end up in a relativistic position, although Nehamas himself thinks that it does not. In this case Nehamas' interpretation also does not do justice to Nietzsche's metaphysics.

Peter Poellner even dedicated his recent study exclusively to the relationship of Nietzsche's perspectivism and his metaphysics [Poellner (1995)]. However, he also came to the conclusion that Nietzsche is putting forward a form of relativism, i.e. his solution to the problem in question is similar to the other two interpretations which were just mentioned: "So it seems that Nietzsche, in effect, concedes that while he believes the apparent metaphysics of the will to power to be 'true for him', it may actually be false (rather than just mistakenly considered to be false) for other subjects or 'perspectives.' Rüdiger Grimm, among others, interprets his pronouncement: 'Nietzsche's scheme can account for both contingencies: it can be both true and false [in his sense] for different individuals at the same time (or the same individual at different times).'

In other words, Nietzsche's view entails a form of relativism." [Poellner (1995): P. 289]. This reply again does not give a satisfactory reply to the question "Why should one believe in Nietzsche's metaphysics, why is it superior, or why does he put it forward?" I will show that Nietzsche does have an adequate reply to that question, and that his metaphysics is not based on a simple form of relativism.

Brian Leiter pointed out that the standard interpretation of perspectivism, which implies that all perspectives are interpretations, leads to too many inconsistencies within Nietzsche's thinking to seriously consider it to be an adequate interpretation of Nietzsche. By representing his critique of the "Received View" (RV) of perspectivism, as he calls it, which is held by such eminent interpreters as Grimm, Kofman, Derrida, Nehamas, Strong, Warnock, Magnus, and Rorty, I think that I will be able to point out some distinctions and clarifications which interpreters have failed to make so far. According to Leiter, the RV is based on the following four claims:

> (i) the world has no determinate nature or structure;
> (ii) our concepts and theories do not 'describe' 'or 'correspond' to this world because it has no determinate character;
> (iii) our concepts and theories are 'mere' interpretations or 'mere' perspectives (reflecting our pragmatic needs, at least in some accounts);
> (iv) no perspective can enjoy an epistemic privilege over any other, because there is no epistemically privileged mode of access to this characterless world. [Leiter (1994): P. 334]

Subsequently, Leiter claims that this is not Nietzsche's position, and then argues for what seems a strange picture of Nietzsche's perspectivism. I will not be concerned with the latter because I think there is too much strong evidence against it which I have already put forward earlier in this book. However, his critique of the RV can provide us with a better understanding of Nietzsche's philosophy as a whole, and enables me to introduce some distinctions previous interpreters of Nietzsche have failed to make.

I think that Leiter's summary of the RV is accurate and that it does represent part of Nietzsche's views, namely, those I have represented in the section called Dionysos. The theses in the Dionysos section are based upon Nietzsche's views presented in the Apollo section. My point is that it is a misrepresentation of Nietzsche's thought to regard the four claims contained in the RV alone. Before considering my solution of the problem in question, I will outline Leiter's critique of the RV.

Leiter points out the problems of interpreters who regard Nietzsche as having put forward what we are calling the RV:

> first, because, they must make it out as an epistemological position worthy of serious attention; and second, they must show how it could be compatible with the rest of his philosophical corpus, which seems unaffected by his radical epistemological doctrine. [Leiter (1994): P. 334]

Leiter is correct in mentioning these questions. Yet, I think that they can be answered. His criticisms of the RV are the following:

> Nietzsche criticises certain views on their epistemic merit, and takes his own view to enjoy an epistemic privilege over those he criticises." [...] Yet, given the RV "there appears to be no room even for Nietzschean criticism (let alone positive claims) having anything to do with epistemic merits. [Leiter (1994): P. 336]

Leiter fails to make the distinction between the superiority of Nietzsche's views with respect to "the truth," and with respect to the spirit of the times. Nietzsche does reject the idea that we can decide upon the superiority of any perspective with respect to "the truth," as I explained in main part two. However, Nietzsche clearly holds that there are hierarchies of perspectives with respect to the spirit of the times. Nietzsche would be foolish, if his philosophy was not able to explain on which basis we decide upon the value or plausibility of a perspective, because human beings clearly always regard some theories as better than others. I will soon clarify the underlying thought behind this reply.

The second main objection Leiter puts forward is the following [Leiter (1994): P. 338]:

> On his view, the world of 'appearing' is just all the world there is—though it is, of course, no longer a 'merely' 'apparent' world. Yet the Received View, by holding that no view gives 'a better picture of the world as it really is' than any other, reinstates the distinction. For on this account there are, on the one hand, epistemically equivalent 'mere' perspectives, and on the other, the indescribable (and hence unknown) world 'as it really is', a world to which no perspective is

> adequate. Hence the paradox: Although Nietzsche rejects the A/R distinction, on the Received View 'mere perspectives' seem to have the same status as the metaphysician's 'mere appearances' that Nietzsche sought to abolish.

However, this paradox does not arise, if one interprets Nietzsche in the way I did. Nietzsche does reject the A/R distinction, and he also holds that no view which a power-constellation can take in, consciously gives "a better picture of the world as it really is." If one bears in mind Nietzsche's artistic metaphysics as represented in Apollo, and also that "the truth" is the sum of all possible perspectives taken together, then it is no problem for Nietzsche to hold both of the former claims. Again I have only alluded to the solution I will put forward to the problems Nietzsche has to face, but these hints should already give an idea of my reply to this problem.

It seems that the problem of consistency within Nietzsche's philosophy, and especially with respect to his views on truth and metaphysics, has been an issue of great perplexity for Nietzsche interpreters so far, and I have not yet come across a convincing solution to them.

3.2.

3.2.1 My Solution (in detail)/Nietzsche

Due to the close link between Nietzsche, the person, and his philosophy, I briefly have to come back to the person Nietzsche to be able to present my solution in detail.

Remember that Nietzsche was brought up as a Christian, then at school came into close contact with Ancient Greek world views, and from that time on believed in the contingency of all world views. Although he held that all world views are contingent, he started interpreting the world in a special way, somewhat related to the way the Greeks used to develop their Apollinian beauties, because it was the Ancient Greek way of thinking which influenced him most in the development of his own world view. It would, however, be false to say that his own philosophy is simply a return to the Ancient Greek way of thinking and living:

> This antithesis of the Dionysian and the Apollinian within the Greek soul is one of the great riddles to which I felt myself drawn when

> considering the nature of the Greeks. Fundamentally, I was concerned with nothing except to guess why exactly Greek Apollinianism had to grow out of a Dionysian subsoil why the Dionysian Greek had to become Apollinian; that is, to break his will to the terrible, multifarious, uncertain, frightful, upon a will to measure, to simplicity, to submission, to rule and concept. The immoderate, disorderly Asiatic lies at his roots; the bravery of the Greek consists in his struggle with his Asiaticism; beauty is not given to him, as little as is logic or the naturalness of customs—it is conquered willed, won by struggle—it is his victory. [WP 1050]

His special way of his seeing the world which he had gradually gained (via his body), provided him with an explanation for the question why a certain type of person developed a certain type of world view. Nietzsche simply could not help but to see the world in the way provided by him by his insights with respect to metaphysics. These insights were that the whole world is will to power, and that all the philosophies and all world views were always brought about by the respective power-constellation they were. Of course, he permitted or rather demanded that the same applies to his own theories as well which becomes clear in the section of BGE cited by Danto. Given that the world is will to power, he also wondered what provides a power-constellation with the greatest power. The greatest power, as we have seen in Apollo is to impose Being on Becoming, to interpret the world in such a way, so that one sees the world of Becoming in a determined way, that is, as a world of Being. Nietzsche's world of Being was constituted out of ER as the form and the Will to power as the content of Being. This world of Being, this artistic metaphysics which I presented as Nietzsche's insights in Apollo were his way of seeing the world, "Nietzsche's truth," as I called it later on. "Nietzsche's truth" of course being separate from "the truth," and also only one interpretation of or hypothesis about the world, as he was well aware: "Supposing that this, too, is only an interpretation—and one will be eager enough to raise this objection. Well—so much the better." This together with what I have said before in Dionysos should make it clear that his conception of the world is also only one interpretation. Still, it is a very special one, as we will soon realise, when I explain why the objection "Why should I believe in it?" cannot be used against him, according to Nietzsche himself.

As I already said in section D, for Nietzsche philosophy is the love of wisdom and not the love of the truth:

> Philosophy as love for wisdom, and so for the wise man as the most fortunate and most powerful who justifies all becoming and would have it recur. Philosophy is not love for men, or for Gods, or for truth; it is love for a certain condition, for a feeling of completion in mind and in senses; it is an affirmation and approval that comes from an overwhelming feeling of shaping power. The high excellence. [KSA Vol. 11, 25 (451), PF]

Wisdom is concerned with values.—the values which one needs to act, to give our lives meaning, sense, stability, because human beings need stability or Being, for human beings cannot stand or bear a completely indeterminate world, as Nietzsche also pointed out [UM 2, 1]. To impose Being on Becoming is the highest power, because one ends up with a world view which also implies values, and which can provide our lives with sense or meaning. Whoever creates values which are accepted creates the face of the world. This is the reason why it provides the creator or inventor of the values (the one who imposes Being on Becoming) with the highest power:

> Not around the inventors of new noise, but around the inventors of new values does the world resolve. [Z "On great Events"]
>
> Around the inventors of new values the world resolves: invisibly it resolves."[Z "On the Flies of the Market"]
>
> Far from the market place and from fame happens all that is great: far from the market place and from fame the inventors of new values have always dwelt. [Z "On the Flies of the Market"]

Nietzsche saw himself as such an inventor of new values by putting forward his interpretation of the world as will to power. He was not someone on the market place who was mainly concerned with his fame while he was alive—but he did aim to be an inventor of a culture, of new values, of a new era. One can see this in section D where I mentioned that Nietzsche is concerned with values rather than with metaphysics, and as we have just seen the world turns around the inventors of new values. This position finds further support in a letter Nietzsche wrote to Overbeck:

> That whole millenia will swear their most solemn oaths in my name—if I do not push things as far as that, then in my own eyes I have achieved nothing. [Nietzsche's letter to Overbeck from the 21.5.1884 in Jaspers (1947): P. 411, PF)

He does not only intend to be a major inventor of values, but he even thinks that he is human being pre-destined to decide upon the values for the forthcoming centuries. The reason why he might be justified in saying that he is the "pre-destined human being" is very problematic, because pre-destination does not seem to fit into his world view. However, at the end of this main part I will put forward some possible explanations for why Nietzsche might have used this expression to refer to himself. The aphorism, in which he mentions this, which says a lot about Nietzsche and his philosophy:

> 1. Great sound of the trumpets; Blessing of the loud tones.
> I am the predestined man, who is determining values for thousands of years to come; a hidden man, a man who has been everywhere, a man without joy, a man who has thrown away from himself everything that is home, everything that brings repose. What constitutes the great style—being master of one's good and bad fortune alike.
>
> 2. The gift I have to offer is able to be received, if those capable of receiving it are there—there is an order for precedence for it. The greatest events are the last to be understood: so I must be a lawgiver.
>
> 3. The time of his appearing: that most dangerous middle period, a time, in which things may go to 'the last man', but also ...; a time characterized by the greatest of all events: God is dead. Only men are still unaware of it, unaware that they are just living on inherited values. The all-pervading neglicence and wastefulness. [KSA vol. 11, 35 (74), PF]

Here, one can clearly see that he thinks of himself as the inventor of new values which will govern the forthcoming millennia. However, that is all I wish to take from this aphorism at the moment. I will definitely come back to it later on, because I think that it contains a lot of material which reveals a lot about himself, his intentions, and his philosophy. Yet, what does Nietzsche have to do to become what he intends to be—the inventor of new values? He has to be convincing, to actually be able to change the perspectives people have onto the world, and he thinks that this is exactly what he can do: "Now I know how, have the know-how, to reverse perspectives: the first reason why a 'revaluation of values' is perhaps possible for me alone." [EH "Why I am so wise" 1]

So far we have got some ideas about what Nietzsche intends to do and also why he wants to do it. He does impose Being on Becoming, he interprets the world in a specific way, and does so mainly for the sake of creating a new system of values. This of course also demands a new metaphysics, although his primary concern are the values. Why does he want to do this? Because his metaphysics and his value system is based upon or rather are his will to power theory. This theory says that all power-constellations aim for power; the one who manages to interpret the world of Becoming as a world of Being has the highest power. By doing exactly this Nietzsche fulfils his own drive for power. He even does so in the best possible way because by imposing Being on Becoming he intended to achieve the highest power possible. Imposing Being on Becoming, of course, is done not primarily for the sake of establishing a metaphysics, but for the sake of acquiring a new value system, since, as we have heard before, the world turns around the creator of new values. Hence, imposing Being on Becoming provides the power-constellation (the person) who does this with the highest possible power. Nietzsche refers to someone who manages to do exactly this as the "highest man":

> Order of rank: He who determines values and directs the will of millenia by giving direction to the highest natures is the highest man. [WP 999]
>
> For the highest man shall also be the highest lord on earth. [Z "Conversation with the Kings"]
>
> I teach: that there are higher and lower men, and that a single individual can under certain circumstances justify the existence of whole millenia—that is, a full, rich, great, whole human being in relation to countless incomplete fragmentary men. [WP 997]
>
> The highest man as legislator of the future [WP 972]

Besides creating the values and the will for millennia, what else, which other characteristics must the highest man have?

> Our insight is the opposite of this: that with every growth of man, his other side must grow too; that the highest man, if such a con-

> cept be allowed, would be the man who represented the antithetical character of existence most strongly, as its sole glory and justification. [WP 881]
>
> Man is beast and superbeast; the higher man is inhuman and superhuman: these belong together. With every increase of greatness and height in man, there is also an increase in depth and terribleness: one ought not to desire the one without the other—or rather: the more radically one desires the one, the more radically one achieves precisely the other. [WP 1027]

So the highest man has to represent the antagonistic character of existence or the unity of opposites in the world, he has to glorify and justify it. This is exactly what Nietzsche himself has done. The will to power metaphysics represents a worldview of permanent Becoming, change and strife. However, this strife culminates in ER which means in Being, in stability, in its direct opposite. His views begin with his artistic metaphysics of stability, order, and harmony, but they end up in a position of perspectivism, denial of "the truth," and nihilism. Again we have both extremes united in one system. So by referring to the highest man, and its qualities, he is referring to himself, perhaps not exclusively, but at least as one among others[34].

Before dealing with the role Nietzsche attributes to himself, his intentions, and his position in the progression of history, I wish to analyse something mentioned a short while ago. Nietzsche thinks that he is able to change perspectives enabling him to bring about a transvaluation of values. If he wishes to change perspectives, then different perspectives must be dominant at present. Nietzsche's view on the history of perspectives dominant in the previous centuries or millennia, can help us understand what he intends to do for the future, why he thinks his position is suitable for the future, in what relation he stands to the previous positions, and how his theories about the progression of history are related to his own philosophy.

3.2.2 Christianity

Christianity is the movement which has dominated the western world in the previous two millennia, according to Nietzsche. So the Christian world view as well as its value system and multiple practices of worship

---

34 The unity of opposites claim plays a very important role in such thinkers as Heraclitus, Dostoevsky, and Jung as well.

have dominated the previous millennia. However, as I have already explained in the section on nihilism, for Nietzsche it is natural for everything which comes into existence to fade out of existence again and vanish. Christianity first had to grow out of its fragile roots to become the multi-national organisation it has been for a long period of time. It grew bigger and bigger, until it started to fade away again at the beginning of the Enlightenment. Decadence then became more and more prominent, and this led to Pessimism, reaching a period of nihilism in the end, out of which something new should be able to grow. We dealt with the stages of this progression in the section nihilism, now we have to apply these insights to the end of Christianity, because, according to Nietzsche, the era of Christianity is completed:

> The time has come when we have to pay for having been Christians for two thousand years: we are losing the centre of gravity by virtue of which we lived; we are lost for a while. Abruptly we plunge into the opposite valuations, with all the energy that such an overvaluation of man has generated in man. [WP 30]
>
> Nihilism stands at the door: whence comes this uncanniest of all guests? ...
>
> The end of Christianity—at the hands of its own morality (which cannot be replaced), which turns against the Christian God ... Skepticism regarding morality is what is decisive. The end of the moral interpretation of the world, which no longer has any sanction after it has tried to escape into some beyond, leads to nihilism. [WP 1]
>
> At the deathbed of Christianity.—Really active people are now inwardly without Christianity, and the more moderate and reflective people of the intellectual middle class now possess only an adapted, that is to say marvelously simplified Christianity. [D 92]
>
> Destiny of Christianity.—Christianity came into existence in order to lighten the heart; but now it has first to burden the heart so as afterwards to be able to lighten it. Consequently it will perish. [HAH 1, 119]
>
> But the struggle against Plato, or, to express it more plainly and for 'the people', the struggle against the Christian—eccesiastical pressure of millenia—for Christianity is Platonism for 'the people'—has created in Europe a magnificent tension of the spirit such as has never existed on earth before: with so tense a bow one can now shoot for the most distant targets ....we good Europeans and free, very free spirits—we have it still, the whole need of the spirit and the whole

> tension of its bow! And perhaps also the arrow, the task and, who knows? the target ... [BGE Preface]

All these excerpts point in the same direction: Christianity is nearly dead, the age of nihilism is at hand. This is no more than a description of what has happened in the previous centuries, according to Nietzsche, but of course it does not yet include an explanation of why this happened. Now we have to bear in mind that with Christianity we have an absolute world view which provided us with answers to all the big questions (value questions, the meaning of life and so on). At the moment we are living in an intermediate period of nihilism. As we earlier realised, nihilism comes about when the absolute world view, previously dominant, no longer appeals to the strength of the majority of the people. The absolute world view can either demand too much or too little of them, in either case it does not appeal to the people anymore and they start to abandon it. So decadence and with it nihilism do not have to be a sign of weakness of the people; they could also mean that the people have become stronger:

> For it could be the precondition of greatness to grow to such an extent in violent tension. Dissatisfaction, nihilism could be a good sign. [WP 111]
>
> Overall insight.—Actually, every major growth is accompanied by a tremendous crumbling and passing away: suffering, the symptoms of decline belong in the times of the tremendous advances; every fruitful and powerful movement of humanity has also created at the same time a nihilistic movement. It could be the sign of a crucial and most essential growth, of the transition to new conditions of existence, that the most extreme form of pessimism, genuine nihilism, would come into the world. This I have comprehended. [WP 112]

At this stage again we find the claim about the unity of opposites within Nietzsche's philosophy of history which is what the highest man manages to represent. Here one can find his claim that growth and decline are always linked; this idea turns up at various places in Nietzsche. He also says that men tend to see opposites in nature, where there are merely differences of degree [HAH 2, 67], or that it is a basic belief of the "metaphysicians" to believe in antagonistic values, whereas he thinks that there are many good reasons to doubt that there are any opposites [BGE 1, 2]. He even says explicitly that in Zarathustra all opposites are connected to a new unity [EH "Thus spoke Zarathustra," 6]. Especially in Zarathustra itself this principle becomes extremely clear:

> Only where there is life is there also will: not will to live but—thus I teach you—will to power .... Verily, I say unto you: good and evil that are not transitory, do not exist. Driven on by themselves, they must overcome themselves again and again. With your values and words of Good and Evil you do violence when you value; and this is your hidden love and the splendor and trembling and overflowing of your soul. But a more violent force and a new overcoming grow out of your values and break egg and eggshell. And whoever must be a creator in good and evil, verily, he must first be an annihilator and break values ... And may everything be broken that cannot brook our truths! There are yet many houses to be built!—Thus spoke Zarathustra. [Z "On Self-Overcoming"]
>
> To esteem is to create: hear this, you creator! ... Through esteeming alone is there value: and without esteeming, the nut of existence would be hollow. Hear this, you creator! Change of values—this is a change of creators. Whoever must be a creator always annihilates ... Good and evil have always been created by lovers and creators ... Zarathustra saw many lands and many peoples. No greater power did Zarathustra find on earth than the works of the lovers: 'good' and 'evil' are their names. [Z "On the thousand and one Goals"]
>
> Fundamental thought: the new values must first be created—we shall not be spared this task! For us the philosopher must be a legislator. New types. (How the highest type hithero (e.g. Greeks) were reared: to will this type of 'chance' consciously). [WP 979]

Here we come across the idea of the unity of creation and destruction and the unity of good and evil. All this confirms our prior hypothesis that when Nietzsche mentioned the higher man, he was including himself in this category. In addition to this we are told that a creator of new values first has to destroy the old ones. This is exactly what Nietzsche did, with vehemence, especially in the "Antichrist," where he used *ad hominem* arguments to make the reader feel uncomfortable about Christianity, linking everything men usually esteem highly, or regard as a positive quality, as something Christianity tries to destroy out of resentment[35]. In his conception one could only be a Christian

35 It is not the case that Nietzsche committed the genetic fallacy by arguing against Christianity, for all his claims are not intended to represent „the truth", as I have stressed in main part 2.

out of weakness, but who wants to be weak? I just wish to hint at his method by citing the following two aphorisms:

> Parasitism as the only practice of the church; with its ideal of anemia, of 'holiness', draining all blood, all love, all hope for life; the beyond as the will to negate every reality; the cross as the mark of recognition for the most subterrenean conspiracy that ever existed—against health, beauty, whatever that has turned out well, courage, spirit, graciousness of the soul, against life itself. This eternal indictment of Christianity I will write on all walls, wherever there are walls—I have letters to make even the blind see. I call Christianity the one great curse, the one great innermost corruption, the one great instinct of revenge, for which no means is poisonous, stealthy, subterranean, small enough—I call it the one immortal blemish of mankind. And time is reckoned from the dies nefastus with which this calamity began—after the first day of Christianity! Why not rather after its last day? After today? Revaluation of all values! [AC 62]
>
> why the notion of another world has always been unfavorable for, or critical of 'this' world—what does this indicate?— ... The places of origin of the notion of 'another world': the philosopher who invents a world of reason, where reasons and the logical functions are adequate: this is the origin of the 'true world'; the religious man who invents a 'divine world': this is the origin of the 'denaturalized, anti-natural' world; the moral man who invents a 'free world': this is the origin of the 'good, perfect, just, holy' world ... The 'other world', as illumined by these facts, as a synonym for nonbeing, nonliving, not wanting to live- ... Consequence: philosophy, religion, and morality are symptoms of decadence. [WP 586]

It seems obvious that people do not wish to become associated with a community which attacks out of resentment beauty, health, life, bravery ... So although Christianity was already declining, Nietzsche tried to hasten this decline by attacking the Christian community by attributing qualities to its members which are not thought very highly of, such as sickliness, and weakness[36]. This attack implicitly contains the new set of values which Nietzsche has created, because health, beauty, life affirmation, and bravery clearly all are abilities, or powers. Whereas resentment, sickness, and so forth, i.e. the qualities he attributes to Christians, are weaknesses. So the metaphysics of the will to power and

36 Nietzsche was not alone in attacking Christianity. Feuerbach, Marx, Freud are some others who were very engaged in that task.

ER which he is building up are already being used by him as a basis in his criticism of Christianity.

The dissolution of the Christian system has been followed by an age of nihilism with exactly the characteristics and brought about in the manner described in the section on nihilism. This age of nihilism probably started with the beginning of the enlightenment and increased in intensity perhaps until the present. Of course, it is difficult to make a judgement about what is going on in one's own time, and I am not inclined to say whether the progression has already reached its peak, or whether this is still to come. Yet, I also do not think this is of great relevance for the present task, because all I am doing is setting out Nietzsche's ideas, but I am not evaluating their worth or their appropriateness.

3.2.3 Science

We need to bear in mind that the age of nihilism is only transitory. It started with the beginning of the enlightenment, was brought about by the loss of the belief in Christianity, and will be transcended at some stage by a new movement. The values for this new movement Nietzsche is attempting to create, believing that his world view will dominate the forthcoming millennia. I will firstly give some characterisation of this new age, then I explain why Nietzsche thinks that it will dominate, and what he has done to make this goal come about.

I have called this section science because Nietzsche's worldview is according to his own criteria a scientific one[37]. By accepting this stipulation I am not implying that Nietzsche's worldview actually corresponds to the way science is dealt with in the twentieth century, but I am not excluding the possibility either. A more specialised study would be required to determine a well founded answer to this question.

Nietzsche was conscious of the fact from fairly early on in his writing career that the next age will be a scientific one. In "Human-all-too-Human," he was already able to see the schemes of the future development: "Now, to be sure, we are still living in science's youthful era." [HAH 1, 257]

Nietzsche scholars might reply that it was only in that (his middle) period that his thinking was scientific. This, however, is an incorrect understanding of Nietzsche, as I will show soon. Here we have to bear

37 Babich gives an excellent overview over the relevance of science within Nietzsche's philosophy [Babich (1994)].

in mind what he said in a letter to Brandes from the fourth of May 1888:

> to see my entire conception from top to bottom, with the immense complex of problems lying, as it were, spread out beneath me, in clear outline and relief. This demands a maximum of power which I scarcely any longer hoped were mine. It all hangs together, for years it had all been on the right track, one builds one's philosophy like a beaver, one is necessary without knowing it. [Nietzsche letter to Brandes in Danto (1965): P. 23]

This provides us with one reason not to reject all of his remarks from his earlier works. Only when Nietzsche's earlier views are blatantly inconsistent with his later positions, should we regard the positions from his earlier works with some suspicion. However, this is not the case with respect to science; although, Nietzsche attributes various meanings to the notion "science," there is one he employs to refer to his own philosophy, and this is the one relevant for my own purposes. I will not analyse the other meanings of the notion "science," but I cite one aphorism as evidence that Nietzsche operated with several meanings of "science": "Any science which attributes a practical significance to itself is not yet a science—for example national economy." [KSA vol. 7, 3 (10), PF]

This aphorism makes it clear that there are many separate forms of science. That there are many different meanings of science should be self-evident, if one takes into consideration how the methods and goals of science have changed throughout the centuries, and the number of meanings of the notion "science" increases even further if we add all the theoretical conceptions of "science"—Nietzsche's own being just one of them. What is Nietzsche's conception of "science"?

> Today we possess science precisely to the extent to which we have decided to accept the testimony of the senses,—to the extent to which we sharpen them further, arm them, and have learned to think them through. [TI "'Reason' in Philosophy" 3]
>
> I observe with astonishment that science has today resigned itself to the apparent world. [WP 583]

These aphorisms tell us that science solely depends on the apparent world, and only trusts human sense perceptions. And for Nietzsche, let us remember, the apparent world is the only real world. There is no other world separate from this one with perfect forms (Plato), "things in themselves" (Kant), or even the "thing in itself" (Schopenhauer). "Science has, moreover, become something very useful for everyone." [D 41]

By promoting science and with it belief in human senses, we promote humanity as well, through development towards the *Uebermensch*. In addition to this, Nietzsche's science is also supposed to transcend Plato's nihilism which is linked to Christianity, and the age of nihilism which dominates the period of time following the Christian era.

According to Nietzsche, science and the Christian religion have never been able to accept each other. Christianity has always used its best weapons to fight science. For example, in its original exposition of the story of Adam and Eve, Christianity was already launching an attack upon science. Science is getting to know something:

> The priest knows only one great danger: that is science, the sound conception of cause and effect. But on the whole science prospers only under happy circumstances—there must be a surplus of time, of spirit, to make 'knowledge' possible. [AC 49]
>
> Has the famous story that stands at the beginning of the bible really been understood? The story of God's hellish fear of science? ...
>
> 'From Woman comes all calamity in the world'—every priest knows that, too. 'Consequently it is from her too that science comes.' Only from woman did man learn to taste of the tree of knowledge. What had happened? The old God was seized with hellish fear. Man had turned out to be his greatest mistake; he had created a rival for himself; science makes godlike—it is all over with priests and gods when man becomes scientific. Moral: science is the forbidden as such—it alone is forbidden. Science is the first sin, the seed of all sin, the original sin. [AC 48]

What is the essential difference between the Christian and the scientific world conception?

> A religion like Christianity, which does not have contact with reality at any point, which crumbles as soon as reality is conceded its rights at even a single point, must naturally be mortally hostile against the 'wisdom of this world', which means science. [AC 47]

Christianity is completely detached from the world, whereas science is linked to the wisdom of the world. What does this mean? We have to bear in mind that Christianity is Platonism for the masses, whereas science only accords credence to the apparent world, the world accessible to the senses. Christianity is essentially dualistic: the world we are living in being of no value, and serving only as a preparation for the next world which has all the value. For science the apparent world becomes the only world, the real world. In addition to this, it is scientific to see the world as the will to survive (as this accords with Darwin's thesis). Although Nietzsche does not regard the theory of the will to survive to be correct, because we do not wish to survive for the sake of the survival, but always to gain something else instead [WP 647; WP 649]. This something else in Nietzsche's case is power. Yet, Nietzsche's will to power theory is very similar to Darwin's will to survival theory (both hold evolutionary theories about the origin of the different species[38]). Therefore Nietzsche also regards himself as justified in seeing his will to power metaphysics as scientific. As his *Uebermensch* theory is closely linked to his will to power metaphysics, there was no need for him to state any further reasons why it is scientific as well. Strength and power in general are qualities science demands and promotes:

> Our air.—We know very well how science strikes those who merely glance at it in passing, as if they were walking by, as women do and unfortunately also many artists: the severity of its service, its inexorability in small as in great matters, and the speed of weighing and judging matters and passing judgement makes them feel dizzy and afraid. Above all they are terrified to see how the most difficult is demanded and the best is done without praise and decorations. Indeed, what one hears is, as among soldiers, mostly reproaches and hard rebukes; for doing things well is considered the rule, and failure is the exception; but the rule always tends to keep quiet. This 'severity of science' has the same effect as the forms and good manners of the best society: it is frightening for the uninitiated. But those who are used to it would never wish to live anywhere else than in this bright, transparent, vigorous, electrified air—in this virile air. [GS 293]

Now it only remains for me to explain why Nietzsche regarded his theory of ER to be scientific—that this is the case he said quite explicitly:

38 Birx gives a clear account of the similarities between Darwin and Nietzsche [Birx (2006), vol. 4, P. 1741-1745].

> Extreme positions are not succeeded by moderate ones but by extreme positions of the opposite kind ... 'The eternal recurrence'... is the most scientific of all possible hypotheses ... There is nothing to life that has value, except the degree of power—assuming that life itself is the will to power. [WP 55]
>
> At that time Nietzsche planned to lapse into silence for the following ten years, in order to make himself ready for the development of the thought of return. [Heidegger (1984): P. 13]

Nietzsche even planned to retreat and remain silent for ten years. This, in his case, does not mean that he did not want to say anything during this period, but that he did not wish to publish a book. Instead he planned to go to Paris or Vienna to study natural sciences in order to be able to prove ER [Andreas-Salome (1994): P. 256—257]. This shows that Nietzsche himself must have taken ER very seriously. We get the same impression if we read what Danto wrote about Nietzsche's attitude towards ER with respect to his relationship to other human beings:

> Overbeck tells us that Nietzsche spoke of it in whispers (as Zarathustra speaks to the dwarf) and alluded to it as an unheard-of revelation. Lou Salome tells of the 'unforgettable moment' when Nietzsche confided this teaching to her 'in a low voice.' Nietzsche himself speaks of the precise time and place—in a place near the towering rock in Sils Maria during august, 1881, —'six thousand feet beyond man and time'—that this idea, which he characterised as 'the highest formula of affirmation that can ever be attained' came to him with the apparent impact of an mystical experience. He was, according to Lou Salome, reluctant to disclose it to the world until he could find the scientific confirmation he thought it must have if it was to be accepted. He regarded it as the 'most scientific of hypotheses.' [Danto (1965): P. 203]

Again I think we can make sense out of his attitude towards ER, if we take into consideration the details of this theory. The way I have set it out in main part 1, ER appeals to the intellect and whatever is scientific has to appeal to the intellect as well. The ER follows from this following line of thought:

> Logic, as a part of the intellect, tells us that the sum total of will to power is either infinite or finite, and that the total number of will to power states in the world is either infinite or finite.

> The intellect does not enable us to think that the sum total of will to power is infinite.
>
> The intellect also does not enable us to think that the total number of will to power states in the world is infinite. Therefore the intellect makes us think that the sum total of will to power is finite and that the total number of will to power states in the world is finite.

Once we have secured these two premises and combined these with Nietzsche's metaphysics, ER follows by necessity. This line of reasoning shows us that we can derive ER by reference to our intellect because whatever appeals to our intellect is scientific. Therefore Nietzsche is justified in referring to ER as the "most scientific of hypotheses."[39]

3.2.4 Spirit

The last remarks should have brought out some essential differences between the Christian world view and Nietzsche's scientific world view; as well it should have cleared up the relationship between Nietzsche's metaphysics and science, and why Nietzsche thinks that his metaphysics can be regarded as scientific.

So far I have mostly focused my attention on Nietzsche's philosophy of the progression of history in this main part. Christianity has governed the previous two millennia. At the beginning of the Enlightenment decadence began, because from then on more and more people started to reject the belief in God, absolute standards, or any form of ideal. The age of nihilism which is just an intermediate period between two ages of absolute standards began. The more the effects of decadence made themselves felt, the more intense and extreme nihilism became. Nietzsche's intention was to create new values which were supposed to govern the forthcoming millennia. This was his intention because, if he managed to do this, then he would have fulfilled his will to power which, according to his own metaphysics, is the basic drive of everything, in the best possible way, and he would have become the highest man. The question we have to answer now is: Why should anyone accept Nietzsche's artistic metaphysics?

---

39 It is interesting to note that all the premises necessary for the ER imply that space is curved. In addition, most of the premises necessary for the ER to occur get support from the perspective of the contemporary natural sciences. The rest of the premises are not regarded as impossible according to the current scientific state of the arts. [Sorgner (2001a), S. 165-170].

This question arises, because, according to Nietzsche in main part two, no perspective (i.e. metaphysics) can correspond to "the truth," because every perspective is necessarily false. Since we cannot get to know "the truth," it is also impossible for us to create a hierarchy of perspectives with respect to "the truth," because there is no basis for us to order different perspectives.

Now I wish to cite the corner stone of my whole interpretation, and essential component for my solution to the main question posed at the start of the book:

> What, then, is the law and belief with which the decisive change, the recently attained preponderance of the scientific spirit over the religious, God-inventing spirit, is most clearly formulated? Is it not: the world, as force, may not be thought of as unlimited, for it cannot be so thought of. We forbid ourselves the concept of an infinite force as incompatible with the concept 'force.' [WP 1062]

The crucial idea in this aphorism is that it expresses Nietzsche's position with respect to the spirit of our times. He says that the majority of people are governed by the scientific spirit, and therewith has defeated the religious spirit which has been dominant over the last two millennia. Nietzsche mentions this distinction at another place to explain why Schopenhauer created his philosophy in the way he did:

> But in our century, too, Schopenhauer's metaphysics demonstrates that even now the scientific spirit is not yet sufficiently strong: so that, although all the dogmas of Christianity have long been demolished, the whole medieval conception of the world and of the nature of man could in Schopenhauer's teaching celebrate a resurrection. [HAH 1, 26]

Both of these aphorisms tell us that even if at the beginning of the nineteenth century the religious spirit was still dominant, its superiority in comparison to the scientific spirit had vanished by the end of the nineteenth century. At this stage I firstly have to clarify what the concept of spirit implies.

> On the three Metamorphoses
>
> Of three metamorphoses of the spirit I tell you: how the spirit becomes a camel; and the camel, a lion; and the lion, finally, a child ...

> What is difficult? asks the spirit that would bear much, and kneels down like a camel wanting to be well loaded ...
>
> All these most difficult things the spirit that would bear much takes upon itself: like the camel that, burdened, speeds into the desert, thus the spirit speeds into its desert.
>
> In the loneliest desert, however, the second metamorphosis occurs: here the spirit becomes a lion who would conquer his freedom and be master in his own desert. Here he seeks out his last master: he wants to fight him and his last God; for ultimate victory he wants to fight with the great dragon.
>
> Who is the great dragon whom the spirit will no longer call lord and god? 'Though shalt' is the name of the great dragon. But the spirit of the lion says 'I will....'.
>
> To create new values—that even the lion cannot do; but the creation of freedom for oneself for new creation—that is within the power of the lion ...
>
> But say, my brothers, what can the child do that even the lion could not do? ...
>
> The child is innocence and forgetting, a new beginning, a game, a self-propelled wheel, a first movement, a sacred 'Yes.' For the game of creation, my brothers, a sacred 'Yes' is needed: the spirit now will his own will, and he who had been lost to the world now conquers his own world.
>
> Of three metamorphoses of the spirit I have told you: how the spirit became a camel; and the camel, a lion; and the lion, finally, a child. [Z "On the Three Metamorphoses"]

I have quoted nearly the whole passage, because it not only elucidates what the spirit is, but also provides further evidence in favour of my interpretation of Nietzsche's philosophy of history. The camel clearly represents the Christians, the lion the nihilists, and the children the philosophers of the future [the creators of new values, willing to experiment—BGE "We scholars," 210—, not believing in "the truth" anymore—BGE "The Free Spirit," 43; KSA vol. 9, 3 (19)].

It depends on the spirit of a person which sort of world view appeals to them. The distinction between religious and scientific spirit corresponds to the distinction between Christianity and science mentioned earlier on. The religious spirit is the spirit of the people who believe in two world theories; the scientific spirit that of the people who believe in their senses and therewith in one world only.

By introducing the religious and the scientific spirit, we get to know two types of spirit. I have already talked about spirit, but only very briefly, when discussing the highest power in Nietzsche's will to power theory. Here I wish to add a couple of remarks about it, for it is essential to know that one has to be in need of spirit to get it, that one loses it again if one does not need it anymore, and that it is closely linked to self-discipline [TI "Skirmishes of an Untimely Man" 14]; its function is the will to give or impose form [WP 658]; it enables human beings to attribute value to sense perceptions a process which is essential for a whole human being [WP 1045]; it enables us to become master of many things [KSA Vol. 11, 34 (131)]; the person who has acquired most of it, is the most powerful one [KSA vol 9, 6 (341)]; it is not distinct from the body [PTG 10 in KSA Vol. 1, 799 (873),]; it provides us with the heart, and the heart gets us excited [KSA vol. 10, 3 (1) 404]. There is much more to be said about the spirit, but for my purposes this enumeration of various qualities associated with spirit should be sufficient.

Which type of spirit one has, however, does not say anything about whether a person belongs to the rule-givers, or the rule-receivers. Whether a person is a rule-giver or rule-receiver depends on the intensity or strength of the respective type of spirit a person has. There are always only very few rule-givers, but many rule-receivers: "that commanding is harder than obeying" [Z "On Self-Overcoming"]

There are only very few who are strong enough to give orders and have the ability to impose form on chaos, who manage to interpret Becoming as Being, and also to make this interpretation appealing to other people. The rule giver has to try to impose the form and order of their own world view on the rule receivers, whose spirit is only formed by those who influence them. Initially, only a few educated people are influenced; these spread the world-view in question further and further, until it is dominant, if it is a succesful world view. Nietzsche, in his own opinion, was just such a rule giver. He not only manages to create such an interpretation, but also claims to have known how to present it appealingly, and even to make it necessary for a period of time:

> The more abstract the truth that one wishes to teach is, the more one must begin by seducing the senses to it. [quoted in Heidegger (1984): P. 35]

> Principle.—An inescapable hypothesis to which humanity must have recourse again and again is more powerful in the long run than the most firmly believed faith in an untruth (the Christian faith, for example). [GS 133]

So Nietzsche tried to seduce our senses by employing metaphors (see Zarathustra) to make his theory appealing. He even tried to make his hypothesis inevitable, because in the second aphorism he was referring to his own theory. On first glance, the latter aphorism might not sound very convincing. Why should an inevitable hypothesis be more powerful in the long run than the strongest held belief in something untrue, e.g. Christianity? Christianity has history and custom in its favour. In addition it is far from clear how a hypothesis can be inevitable?

Nietzsche's hypothesis is inevitable, according to himself, as I will show now. I have already explained why Nietzsche thinks that his interpretation of the world is scientific. In addition to this, he also thinks that the scientific spirit has finally defeated the religious spirit[40] which implies for him that he expects more and more people to see the world on the basis of the scientific spirit. And this means that they believe that there is only the world of appearance, that an evolutionary account of the development of organisms is accurate, and that a rather physical view about the progression of the universe is correct. Yet, if Nietzsche's theory is scientific and presented in such a way that it appeals to the people, and if the majority of people are governed by the scientific spirit, then Nietzsche is justified in expecting that his own hypothesis about the world is inevitable and will govern the following centuries. What it means for his world view to dominate the following centuries, and whether he has actually achieved what he was aiming for are different issues.[41]

---

40 This change with respect to the governing spirit also implies that the people have become stronger and therefore that the nihilism we are living in is an active nihilism, for the scientific spirit presupposes more strength in human beings than the religious spirit.

41 I personally think that he even might have achieved what he was aiming for. All the philosophers of Post-modernism can be seen as the personification of Nietzsche's philosophers of the future. They all agree to Nietzsche's denial of „the truth" or the death of God. Nietzsche is the Father of Postmodernism, for he has initiated the beginning of a new era—the era of the loss of truth. The postmodern philosophers also aim for power,

One should bear in mind at this stage that he did not create the worldview which appeals to the people in order to appeal to the people, but created it because it was a necessity for him to see the world from such a perspective: "There was no psychology at all before me.—To be the first here may be a curse; it is at any rate a destiny." [EH "Why I am a destiny" 6]

Nietzsche, of course, does not want to please the herd. Yet, he expects the herd to accept his conception of the world in the long run. This is no more than a necessary consequence of Nietzsche's belief that the scientific spirit will govern the following millennia, that his hypotheses are scientific, and that he is able to change perspectives. If all this turned out to be correct, Nietzsche would actually have become the inventor of a new age, and with that the highest man, the centre of the new world. In this way, he could fulfil his will to power in the best possible way. The masses are only a means for him to fulfil his natural drive for the highest power. "Basic error: to place the goal in the herd and not in single individuals! The herd is a means, nothing more!" [WP 766]

It is obvious that this is a more Nietzschean position than if one held that Nietzsche just created his world view to please the masses or the herd. After the discussion about the two types of spirit, it should be clear how to answer the question: In what respect is his world view superior to all the others? It appeals to the spirit of the times of the present and near future, and the spirit of the times is the scientific spirit. Nietzsche's world view appeals to this scientific spirit, because it is very scientific. His will to power theory is an improved version of Darwin's theory, and ER appeals to the intellect (for science always appeals to the intellect). The intellect comprises logic and the categories of reason, and it provides us with "our truth," e.g. we cannot help thinking in its given limits. However, even if the intellect provides us with "our truth" at the moment, it has not necessarily always done so. "Our truth" is only "our truth" for a certain period of time, just as the scientific spirit will govern or the religious spirit has governed human thinking only for a certain period of time. Yet, because Nietzsche thinks that the scientific spirit will govern the judgements of human beings in the near future, and that Nietzsche's theory appeals to this way of thinking, human beings are and will be bound to regard it as superior. This means that after the age

---

by trying to impose their own forms on Being, while denying that they are putting forward the only possible solution. One should not underestimate Nietzsche's influence on hermeneutics, existentialism, and deconstruction.

of Christianity, and the intermediary age of nihilism, Nietzsche expects the age of science to be dominant for a significant period of time.

2.2.5 Tragedy, Dionysos & the Crucified

The age of science is linked to a tragic outlook on life. The claim that a tragic world view can be combined with the scientific one is opposed to Nietzsche's views on science in Ancient Greece. In that era he regarded scientific thinking to be related to a form of optimism. I am even tempted to say that in Nietzsche, his own prediction of the "Birth of Tragedy" came true[42]:

> and only after the spirit of science has been pursued to its limits, and its claim to universal validity destroyed by the evidence of these limits may we hope for a rebirth of tragedy—a form of culture for which we should have to use the symbol of the music-practicing Socrates in the sense spoken above. [BT 17]

Socrates in the "Birth of Tragedy" was linked to the scientific way of thinking and music was linked to tragedy. So, the music-making Socrates with whom the rebirth of tragedy comes about is fulfilled through Nietzsche. Nietzsche is the music-making Socrates. Nietzsche is proclaiming this tragic age of Europe [WP 864], and that *incipit tragoedia* [GS 342] by which he refers to his own world view as the dominant one. It is the ability to affirm all the terrors of life, to say yes to life, to reach an amor fati which is linked to the beginning of a tragic age, for it is the sign of strength that a tragic age comes about. All this is what Nietzsche is describing in his own world view. Especially ER is the best test whether one can affirm life, and say Yes to life. It is a matter of strength to hold ER, without it being the reason for one's own destruction, because the person in question must accept that everything that has happened to him and will happen to him will happen to him an infinite amount of times. So someone who accepts ER and can stand it, expresses this person's capability for the highest affirmation of life. This thought is linked with the concept of the *amor fati*, but a more detailed treatment of this topic would lead me too far astray. All I wished to show here was the relation between Nietzsche's metaphysics, saying Yes to one's life, and the tragic age:

42 I have explained this in detail in a separate article [Sorgner (2004a), P. 91-113].

> I promise a tragic age: the highest art in saying Yes to life, tragedy, will be reborn when humanity has eathered the consciousness of the hardest but most necessary wars without suffering from it. [EH "The Birth of Tragedy 4]
>
> Pleasure in tragedy characterizes strong ages and natures. [WP 852]

Accepting life, saying Yes to life, given ER, is the highest form of life affirmation. Once the people have the strength to bear such a world view, and Nietzsche thinks that human beings are starting to acquire the appropriate strength, the new tragic era or the age of science will begin. This is also supposed to be the time when tragedy as a form of art is supposed to be reborn in its proper manner.

Nietzsche's philosophy and his way of thinking in general is very similar to the scheme of Ancient Greek tragedy. This should not surprise us, however, since his philosophy originates in his reflections on the Apollinian and the Dionysian force in Ancient Greece. Tragedy finds its source in the Dionysian celebrations in Ancient Greece, and it is possible that originally all tragedies were adaptations of the story of Dionysos. Ancient tragedy is constituted from the interplay between two groups; the chorus on the one side, and the actors on the other. Originally there was only the chorus; tragedy began when the first actor or protagonist was selected to present his individual character. Gradually, more and more individual actors were permitted to interact on stage. The chorus represents the Dionysian unity of the world, and the individual actors the Apollinian creations. In Ancient tragedies the scenes were alternatively dominated by chorus and individual actors, i.e. the plot consisted of a permanent interplay between Dionysos and Apollo or destruction and creation. We can find this distinction again in Nietzsche's philosophy: the age of nihilism is related to Dionysos and the age of science to Apollo. This distinction is my inspiration for the headings of the first and the second main part of my book.

However, we could also transform this insight to another higher level. In that case, we can find the distinction between theories including a believe in "the truth," as Christianity, and others which do not belief in "the truth," e.g. Nietzsche's philosophy, his Apollo (age of science) plus his Dionysos (age of nihilism). In this case, Apollo and Dionysos formed a new higher unity which one could also refer to as 'Dionysos', standing for a model which does not believe in "the truth." This 'Dionysos' would have the Christian world view with its belief in "the truth" as its counterpart with the name 'Apollo.' Again, this time at a higher level, we can find the tragic interplay between Apollo and Dionysos in Nietzsche's way of thinking.

I think that the basic thought behind this interpretation should have come across at this stage. This example shows that one can see 'Dionysos' as having two different meanings. Firstly, it can relate only to the destructive force[43]. Secondly, 'Dionysos' can also refer to the process of destruction and creation, as in the case of Greek tragedies. As the Ancient tragedies were being performed in honour of Dionysos, his name contained both forces—the chorus (Dionysos, destruction) as well as the individual protagonists (Apollo, creation). This meaning of 'Dionysos', which includes the destructive and the creative force, is the meaning Nietzsche uses in his later writings.

In light of this Nietzsche regards himself as justified in referring to himself as the last disciple of Dionysos in his later writings.

> "Saying Yes to life even in its strangest and hardest problems, the will to life rejoicing over its own inexhaustibility even in the very sacrifice of its highest types—that is what I called Dionysian, that is what I guessed to be the bridge to the psychology of the tragic poet ... I, the last disciple of the philosopher Dionysos." [TI "What I owe to the Ancients" 5]
>
> "The affirmation of passing away and destroying, which is the decisitive feature of a Dionysian philosophy; saying Yes to opposition and war; becoming" [EH "The Birth of Tragedy" 3]
>
> "I, the last disciple and initiate of the God Dionysos" [BGE "What is noble?" 295]
>
> "I am a disciple of the philosopher Dionysos; I should prefer to be even a satyr to being a saint." [EH Preface 2]

However, Nietzsche, the disciple of Dionysos, is also the Antichrist:

> It was against morality that my instinct turned with this questionable book, long ago; it was an instinct that aligned itself with life and that discovered for itself a fundamentally opposite doctrine and valuation of life—purely artistic and Anti-Christian. What to call it?

---

43 This is the meaning it has in this book when I employ it as a heading for main part two, and it is also the meaning Nietzsche used in the „Birth of Tragedy".

> As a philologist and man of words I baptised it, not without taking some liberty—for who could claim to know the rightful name of the Antichrist?—in the name of a Greek God: I called it Dionysian. [BT "Attempt at a Self-Criticism" 5]
>
> I am, in Greek, and not only in Greek, the Antichrist." [EH "Why I write such good books" 2]

Nietzsche regards himself as the Antichrist. Who is the Antichrist? According to the Bible: "For many deceivers have gone out into the world, men who will not acknowledge the coming of Jesus Christ in the flesh; such a one is the deceiver and the Antichrist" (2 Jn, 7). "Children, it is the last hour; and as you have heard that Antichrist is coming, so now many Antichrists have come; therefore we know that it is the last hour." (Jn 2, 18) "Who is the liar but he who denies that Jesus is the Christ? This is the Antichrist, he who denies the father and the son." (Jn 2, 22) "every spirit which confesses that Jesus Christ has come in the flesh is of God, and every spirit which does not confess Jesus is not of God. This is the spirit of Antichrist, of which you heard that it was coming, and now it is in the world already." (Jn 4, 2-3) [All Bible quotes taken from ed. Lindsell (1971)]. All these descriptions apply to Nietzsche himself, and he says explicitly that he assumes the counter position to Christianity, since for him Platonism is Christianity for the masses, and his philosophy is inverted Platonism:

> My philosophy is inverted Platonism: the further you are away from 'true Being,' the clearer, fairer and better it all is. My goal—life as in appearances. [KSA vol. 7, 7 (156), PF]
>
> for Christianity is Platonism for 'the people' [BGE Preface]

In addition to this he has written a Gospel for the future as he himself says:

> For one should not make a mistake about the meaning of the title that this gospel of the future wants to bear. 'The will to power: Attempt at a Revaluation of all Values'—in this formulation a countermovement finds expression, regarding both principle and task; a movement that in some future will take the place of this perfect nihilism—but presupposes it, logically and pychologically, and certainly can come only after and out of it. For why has the advent of nihilism become necessary? Because the values we have had hithero thus draw their

> final consequence; because nihilism represents the ultimate logical conclusion of our great values and ideals—because we must experience nihilism before we can find out what value these 'values' really had.—We require, sometime, new values. [WP 4]

The similarity between Christianity and Nietzsche's philosophy becomes even more obvious if we take "Thus spoke Zarathustra" into consideration, because it is very similar to parts of the New Testament (i.e. the Gospels). All four parts of Zarathustra are mainly about Zarathustra, in the same way as all four Gospels are about Jesus Christ (New Testament: three parts by synoptic writers, one was separate—John. Zarathustra: Three parts written around the same time, one much later). One might even go so far as to compare Nietzsche's works published before the Zarathustra with the Old Testament and the ones after Zarathustra with the New Testament. In the same way as the style in the Bible varies immensely from piece to piece, Nietzsche employs very many different styles. Nietzsche writes poetry as in the Song of Songs, and parables as in the Gospels. In addition, the Bible like Nietzsche's work is filled with metaphors, and symbols. Both works employ the art of the mythology of numbers. A fascinating discussion about the mythology of numbers in Nietzsche can be found in Claus-Arthur Scheier's article "The Rationale of Nietzsche's Genealogy of Morals" [Scheier (1994): P. 449-459]:

> For note that the Genealogy is divided into three parts containing, seventeen, twenty-five, and twenty-eight aphorisms respectively, the sum total thus amounting to seventy—precisely the number of chapters of Zarathustra 1—3 (including the sections of the Prologue). At first glance this might seem to be accidental, or, in any case, irrelevant. But there are many examples of the fact that Nietzsche loved to count his books and their parts, chapters, aphorisms, and, in the case of Zarathustra, even the verses. Notoriously his favourite numbers were ten and seven—the latter presumably because of the New Testament book of revelation, the former because of the Old Testament Decalogue and the Dekas of the Phythagoreans. In this light it is not far fetched to discover that the rationale of the seemingly irrational division of the Genealogy is the golden section, first applied to the complex as a whole, and then to its greater part—a device Nietzsche might have thought of before, but had never used in print.

Something else should make us incline to reconsider Nietzsche's intentions even more. In "The Antichrist," one can find a "Decree against Christianity," in which he not only replaces the Ten Commandments of Christianity with Seven of his own, but also proclaims the introduction of a new time calculation, remembering that if we say today is the 4.5.1998 we still calculate our time with respect to the birth of Jesus Christ, and therefore Christian belief is somehow even implicit in our time calculation only. He wants a clean break with Christianity, and thinks that in order for us to achieve this, we need to introduce a new time calculation:

> Decree against Christianity
> Proclaimed on the first day of the year one (on September 30, 1888 of the false time scheme)
> War to the death against depravity: depravity is Christianity ...
> The Antichrist

All this seems to imply that Nietzsche rejects and even despises Christianity. However, I wonder whether this is the only inference or even the best we can make, using the given premises. Should we not consider which role the Antichrist plays in the Bible? Should not we bear in mind the Revelation, if we read the following passage by Nietzsche?

> "1. *Great sound of the trumpets*; Blessing of the loud tones.
> I am the predestined man, who is determining values for thousands of years to come; a hidden man, a man who has been everywhere, a man without joy, a man who has thrown away from himself everything that is home, everything that brings repose. What constitutes the great style—being master of one's good and bad fortune alike.
>
> 2. The gift I have to offer is able to be received, if those capable of receiving it are there—there is an order for precedence for it. The greatest events are the last to be understood: so I must be a lawgiver.
>
> 3. The time of his appearing: that most dangerous middle period, a time, in which things may go to 'the last man', but also ...; a time characterized by the greatest of all events: God is dead. Only men are still unaware of it, unaware that they are just living on inherited values. The all-pervading negligence and wastefulness." [KSA vol. 11, 35 (74), PF]

What can we read in the Revelations 8-11? Cannot one hear the same trumpets there—*the great sound of trumpets* Nietzsche mentioned in the last aphorism? And we also should not forget the beast 666:

> "The seven *trumpets*
> 1. The first *trumpet* .....8. The seventh *trumpet*"
> These are of one mind and give over their power and authority to the beast; they will make war on the Lamb." [Lindsell (1971): Rev 17, 13-14]

Does not Nietzsche stress exactly this (the beast making war on the lamb), when he writes:

> Have I been understood?—Dionysos versus the Crucified ... [EH "Why I am a Destiny" 9]
> Why did life, physiological well-constitutedness everywhere succumb? ...Dionysos versus 'the Crucified'.. The strong and the weak: the healthy and the sick; the exception and the rule. There is no doubt who is the stronger ... [WP 401]
> Dionysos versus the 'Crucified': there you have the antithesis. It is not a difference in regard to their martyrdom—it is a difference in the meaning of it ... One will see that the problem is that of the meaning of suffering: whether a Christian meaning or a tragic meaning of suffering ...[WP 1052]
> to overcome everything Christian through something supra-Christian, and not merely to put it aside—for the—Christian doctrine was the counterdoctrine to the Dionysian; [WP 1051]

The question which arises for me is not the one which traditionally comes to mind for the standard interpreters. One used to see Nietzsche only as the philosopher, psychologist, and artist who attacked, rejected and despised Christianity who did not wish to have anything to do with it any more—but is this correct? The parables he wrote, the metaphors he used, the styles he wrote in, the expressions he used to refer to himself as well as others, the philosophy of the progression of history which he has been putting forward—all this provides one with reasons to interpret him differently from how one used to. I am not denying that Nietzsche is rejecting Christianity, and puts forward a world view based on the importance of appearance, a new ontology of ER and the will to power—but still I wonder whether this is not the result of another deeper belief within himself. Nietzsche refers to himself as the Antichrist, and does everything to create his own philosophy as an inverted version of Platonism which, according to him, is the intellectual version of Christianity. Nietzsche with his methods of style of expression remains within the Christian tradition. This makes me ask the question: Does not Nietzsche in referring to himself as the Antichrist, in addition to all the other things he does, make himself fit into the Christian world view? Is not he himself part of the Christian scheme? He says that he is a predestined human being—does this pre-destination arise out of a divine necessity—even under his own decree? Does he not have to have accepted the Christian metaphysics by doing all that he has done?

One could even go so far as to ask: Is Nietzsche a Christian?

I am defining a Christian as a person who believes in the Christian metaphysics, but this leaves open the question of worship. It is pretty clear that Nietzsche does not worship the Christian God. Still might he not believe in this God? Might he accept that he will be damned for being the person he is or even has to be?

I will leave this question open to further investigation. All I was aiming to do in this last main part I have done. I have explained why Nietzsche put forward his own philosophy, although he regards it to be as false as every other perspective—namely because it appeals to the spirit of the present and future times, according to him. In this way I have managed to answer a question which has puzzled many eminent commentators.

Conclusion

This brief, last chapter provides me with some space to stress what I have tried to convey with this study, namely that Nietzsche had good reasons to put forward his philosophy even though he said that it is not true. Danto, Nehamas, and Poellner did not grant Nietzsche this position. They claimed that all of Nietzsche's claims are merely his own truth. Yet, I hope that I have managed to show that this is not the case. Nietzsche did not regard his philosophy to be only his own truth. He thought that it would be dominant in forthcoming millennia because human beings will have become more powerful, their spirit longs for a more demanding theory, and his philosophy is suitable for this purpose. Nietzsche's philosophy appeals to the scientific spirit which will govern the forthcoming centuries. This claim also explains why Nietzsche is not inconsistent in holding that all perspectives are equally false with respect to "the truth," but that his philosophy is superior to others, it is so because it appeals to the spirit of the times, i.e. the scientific spirit. So according to Nietzsche, the age of science began with himself. This is the thought advanced at the end of my last chapter. However, it is also a thought with which another discussion could begin. I only put forward an exegesis of certain aspects of Nietzsche's thought, yet on the basis of this exegesis one could ask how plausible Nietzsche's account appears to oneself. Heidegger would have said that Nietzsche was right in what he said about science, given my exegesis. "Technology, we are told, is 'a destiny within the history of Being', its latest and perhaps most enduring phase, and one which, in the shape of national economic self-aggrandisement, 'completes' a longer standing tendency towards 'subjectivity's unconditioned self-assertion' (BW 220 f)." [Cooper (1996): P. 54]

What do I think of Nietzsche's claims? I do not agree with Nietzsche's metaphysics. My reasons for this I will state in another study[44]. However,

44 Inmy article "Narzißmus und Nietzsches Wille zur Macht," I criticise Nietzsche using his own method. Thereby, I state reasons why the will to power is not the only basic drive of human beings [Sorgner (2001b), P. 249-254]. The article also gives hints towards what I regard as another fundamental drive—the will to love. The will to love, and the will to power, or in less anthropomorphic terminology, the drive towards unity, and the drive towards singularity seem to me to be two basis human drives. Wagner in his tetralogy "The Ring of the Nibelung" agrees with this interpretation,

I am very sympathetic towards his philosophy, and grateful to Nietzsche for making me aware of the importance of power and stability.

as therein power and love are shown to be the two fundamental human drives. The importance of love and power was also stressed by T. K. Seung in his recent book "Goethe, Nietzsche, and Wagner: Three Spinozan Epics of Love and Power" [2006].

Appendix

I feel obliged to dedicate an appendix to a philosopher, whom I have hardly ever mentioned within this book, but of whom one can be reminded very often when one reads my interpretation of Nietzsche's philosophy. The philosopher I have in mind is Hegel. Due to the close relationship with respect to time, location and ideas of these two philosophers, at this stage I feel obliged to mention some of the most important similarities and dissimilarities of Nietzsche's thought to that of Hegel. It is astonishing how closely related the concepts of these two philosophers are. The first point which is to mention are their philosophies of history. Hegel was the first to introduce the historical nature of our knowledge. According to him, the process of the development of knowledge is a determinate one. One stage follows onto the other by necessity. His philosophy is a teleology, so the process of history aims for an end which in Hegel is absolute knowledge. It is reached, when the absolute has managed to comprehend itself, and with it the absolute idea. The absolute idea contains every determinateness and it "alone is being, imperishable life, self-knowing truth, and the whole of truth" [Singer (1983): P. 80]. Absolute knowledge is "spirit knowing itself as spirit," for reality is constituted by spirit. Ultimately, there is only one universal spirit, and all the individual spirits are to a greater or lesser degree part of it. The determinate way of progression toward this aim (spirit comprehending itself) in Hegel can be described in an abstract way by his dialectical logic which says that the movement progresses from the tension between the thesis and the antithesis towards their synthesis. In some cases the synthesis can then be taken as another thesis, with which the process starts anew. The very final synthesis is absolute knowledge.

This brief outline of Hegel's main ideas reveals to us that there are some striking similarities between Hegel's philosophy and my interpretation of Nietzsche's thought. The two most significant points are the importance of spirit and historical nature of knowledge in both thinkers. However, one should not take the similarities too far. Hegel's account of the historical progression is teleological, whereas Nietzsche's is circular. The underlying rationality in Hegel's progression of history can be described with his dialectical logic, whereas in Nietzsche it can only be said that the will to power brought about the change of the dominant world views. Here a Hegelian might object that in my interpretation of Nietzsche the scientific age which follows onto the Christian age is the inverted version of the latter, so Hegel's dialectical logic applies to this description of the historical progression as well. This, however, is not the case. Firstly, it is the intermediate age of nihilism which follows immediately onto the age of Christianity. If the Hegelian says that, in this case, this age can also be seen as an application of the dialectical logic of Hegel, then Hegel's dialectical logic is simply an empty term to explain whatever progression actually takes place (Schopenhauer makes a nice point, when he says that Hegel's philosophy proves that whatever exists exists). Secondly, in case we do not wish to let the age of nihilism count as a separate age, for it is only an intermediate position, then I could still reply that the age of science is not the only possible inverted version of the age of Christianity, but only one possible inverted version of it. It is one interpretation which portrays itself as the inverted version of the formerly dominant world interpretation, but is only one among many. In this case again, if the Hegelian claimed that Hegel's dialectical logic still applies, it would have to be regarded as empty, for it is arguable that any two ages can be interpreted as being antagonistic.

The similarities of Hegel and Nietzsche with respect to the importance of spirit in both of their works should not be taken too far either. Firstly, Hegel believes that the absolute can actually comprehend itself (spirit can know itself as spirit) and it even has comprehended itself within the last sections of his Phenomenology. Thereby, he claims to have established the truth with his philosophy, and the truth is connected with the universal spirit. However, as we have seen Nietzsche does not claim to put forward "the truth," thinks that "the truth" is not desirable and is ugly, and that it is impossible to get to know "the truth." The different kinds of spirit, which turn up in Nietzsche (religious spirit, scientific spirit), and the various forms within each spirit, are all different kinds falsifications. Although he refers to them as "*truth*'s," they are necessarily distinct from "the truth," for all "*truth*'s" are different with respect to "the truth" and are falsifications. So, whereas in Hegel spirit is always linked to the truth, it is linked to a kind of falsification in Nietzsche. However, one might be tempted to argue that in Hegel it is only the universal spirit which is linked to the truth, and that it is the same conception in Nietzsche, for "the truth" in Nietzsche is constituted out of all perspectives taken together in one organism. So the only difference between Hegel and Nietzsche would be that in Hegel human beings can grasp the truth, whereas in Nietzsche they cannot. This, however, oversimplifies the discussion, because in Hegel only human beings can have spirit, but in Nietzsche it is a universal phenomena, for whenever I mention "mind" in my interpretation of Nietzsche I just refer to a special type of spirit, which enables organisms to form their perspective, as it gives organisms a basis for making evaluations.

Abstract

The book deals with the question: Is there any good reason to believe in Nietzsche's metaphysics even though he himself claims that it is not "the truth" in correspondence with the world? The traditional replies given by Danto, Nehamas, and Poellner are that Nietzsche's metaphysics is only valid for Nietzsche himself, and they, thereby, turned his philosophy into a form of relativism. However, this answer does not take into consideration Nietzsche's claim for the general superiority of his philosophy. In addition, Nietzsche's view seems inconsistent—on the one hand he claimed all perspectives are equally false with respect to "the truth," but on the other hand he regarded his views as superior. I explain in which respect Nietzsche justifies his claims, that Nietzsche's position is not inconsistent, and why consistency is important for him.

In the first chapter, I present Nietzsche's metaphysics of the will to power and the eternal recurrence of everything.

In the second chapter, I show how Nietzsche's metaphysics led him to his perspectivism, i.e. that all views are interpretations, his denial of "the truth," that all perspectives are equally false with respect to "the truth," that it is essential for human beings to have a defined perspective (e.g. to have a consistent worldview) and his presentation of nihilism. These claims, however, seem to contradict the claims in the main part one.

In chapter three, I explain why Nietzsche thinks that his metaphysics will come to be regarded as superior for a certain period of time, as transcending the long dominant but declining world-view of Christianity. The claim for the superiority of his philosophy is supported by the belief not that it is true, but that it contains elements which will appeal to people in the future.

Bibliography

Primary Literature

Nietzsche, Friedrich "Kritische Studienausgabe" (KSA) edited by Giorgio Colli and Mazzino Montinari (Munich: Deutscher Taschenbuch Verlag GmbH & Co. KG, 1967-1977).

Nietzsche, Friedrich "On the Genealogy of Morals; Ecce Homo" translated from the German by Walter Kaufmann (New York: Random House, Inc., 1967)

Nietzsche, Friedrich "The Portable Nietzsche" selectet and translated from the German by Walter Kaufmann (New York: The Viking Press, Inc., 1954)

Nietzsche, Friedrich "The Gay Science" translated from the German by Walter Kaufmann (New York: Random House, Inc., 1974)

Nietzsche, Friedrich "Human, All too Human" translated from the German by R. J. Hollingdale (Cambridge: Cambridge University Press, 1996)

Nietzsche, Friedrich "Beyond Good and Evil" translated from the German by R. J. Hollingdale (London: Penguin Books Ltd., 1973)

Nietzsche, Friedrich "Untimely Meditations" translated from the German by R. J. Hollingdale (Cambridge: Cambridge Univerrsity Press, 1983)

Nietzsche, Friedrich "Daybreak" translated from the German by R. J. Hollingdale (Cambridge: Cambridge University Press, 1982)

Nietzsche, Friedrich "The Birth of Tragedy; The Case of Wagner" translated from the German by Walter Kaufmann (New York: Random House, Inc., 1967)

Nietzsche, Friedrich "The Will to Power" translated from the German by Walter Kaufmann and R. J. Hollingdale (London: Weidenfeld and Nicholson, 1968)

Secondary Literature

Abel, Günter "Nietzsche: Die Dynamik des Willens zur Macht und die ewige Wiederkehr" second edition (Berlin, New York: De Gruyter, 1998)

Andreas-Salomè, Lou "Friedrich Nietzsche in seinen Werken" (Frankfurt am Main: Insel Verlag, 1994)

Babich, Babette E. "Nietzsche's Philosophy of Science: Reflecting Science on the Ground of Art and Life" (New York: State Univ. of New York Press, 1994)

Beardsley, Monroe C. "Aesthetics from Classical Greece to the Present: A Short History" (London: The University of Alabama Press, 1966)

Birx, H. James. "Nietzsche" " in Birx, H. James (Ed.) "Encyclopedia of Anthropology" in 5 vol. (Thousan Oaks, California: Sage Publications, 2006), vol. 4, P. 1741-1745.

Budd, Malcolm "Music and the Emotions: The Philosophical Theories" (London: Routledge & Kegan Paul, 1992)

Camus, Albert "The Rebel" translated from the French by Anthony Bower (London: Penguin, 1962)

Camus, Albert "Der Mythos von Sisyphos" translated from the French by Hans Georg Brenner und Wolf Dietrich Rasch (Düsseldorf: Karl Rauch Verlag GmbH, 1956)

Clark, Maudemarie "Nietzsche: On Truth and Philosophy" (Cambridge: Cambridge University Press, 1990)

Cooper, David E. "Heidegger" (London: The Claridge Press, 1996)

Danto, Arthur "Nietzsche as Philosopher" (New York: Columbia University Press, 1965)

Ellenberger, Henri "The Discovery of the Unconscious" (New York: Fontana Press, 1970)

Grayling, A. C. (Ed.) "Philosophy: A Guide through the Subject" (Oxford: Oxford University Press, 1995)

Grimm, Rüdiger Hermann "Nietzsche's Theory of Knowledge" (Berlin: Walter de Gruyter, 1977)

Hamlyn, David Walter " Schopenhauer" (London: Routledge & Kegan Paul Ltd., 1980)

Heidegger, Martin "Nietzsche" 2 vol. (Pfullingen: Verlag Günther Neske, 1961)

Heidegger, Martin "Nietzsche vol. 1" translated from the German by David Farrell Krell, San Francisco: Harper & Row, Publishers, 1979)

Heidegger, Martin "Nietzsche vol.2," translated from the German by David Farrell Krell (San Francisco: Harper & Row, Publishers, 1984)

Hondrich, Ted (Ed.) "The Oxford Companion to Philosophy" (Oxford: Oxford University Press, 1995)

Hume, David "A Treatise of Human Nature" (Oxford: Clarendon Pree, 1967)

Jaspers, Karl "Nietzsche: Einführung in das Verständnis seines Philosophierens" (Berlin: Walter de Gruyter & Co., 1947)

Jackson, Robert Louis "Dialogues with Dostoevsky" (Stanford, California: Stanford University Press, 1993)

Kaufmann, Walter "Nietzsche: Philosopher, Psychologist, Antichrist" 4thed. (Princeton: Princeton University Press, 1974)

Leiter, Brian "Perspectivism in Nietzsche's Genealogy of Morals" in Schacht, Richard (Ed.) "Nietzsche, Genealogy, Morality" (Berkeley, Los Angeles, London: University of California Press, 1994), P. 334-357.

Lermontov, Mikhail "A Hero of our Times" translated from the Russian by Paul Foote (London: Penguin Books, 1966)

Lindsell, Harold (Ed.) "Study Bible" Revised Standard Version 2nd. ed. (Cambridge: Cambridge University Press, 1971]

Müller-Lauter, Wolfgang "Nietzsche: Seine Philosophie der Gegensätze und die Gegensätze seiner Philosophie" (Berlin: Walter de Gruyter & Co., 1971)

Nehamas, Alexander "Nietzsche: Life as Literature" (Cambridge/Mass.: Harvard University Press, 1985)

Owen, David "Nietzsche, Politics & Modernity" (London: Sage Publications Ltd., 1995)

Parkes, Graham (Ed.) "Nietzsche and Asian Thought" (Chicago: University of Chicago Press, 1991)

Poellner, Peter "Nietzsche and Metaphysics" (Oxford: Clarendon Press, 1995)

Quine, W. V. O. "From a Logical Point of View" (Cambridge. Mass.: Harvard University Press, 1953)

Rorty, Richard "Philosophy and the Mirror of Nature" (Oxford: Princeton University Press, 1980)

Rorty, Richard "Contingency, Irony, and Solidarity" (Cambridge: Cambridge University Press 1989)

Schacht, Richard "Nietzsche" (London: Routledge & Kegan Paul, 1983)

Schacht, Richard (Ed.) "Nietzsche, Genealogy, Morality" (Berkeley, Los Angeles, London: University of California Press, 1994)

Scheier, Claus-Artur "The Rationale of Nietzsche's *Genealogy of Morals*" in Schacht, Richard (Ed.) "Nietzsche, Genealogy, Morality" (Berkeley, Los Angeles, London: University of California Press, 1994), P. 449-459.

Schopenhauer, Arthur "Ueber die vierfache Wurzel des Satzes vom zureichenden Grunde; Ueber den Willen in der Natur" (Zürich: Diogenes Verlag AG, 1977)

Seung, T. K. "Goethe, Nietzsche, Wagner: Three Spinozan Epics of Love and Power" (Oxford: Lexington Books, 2006)

Simmel, Georg "Philosophie der Mode; Die Religion; Kant und Goethe;

Simmons, Scott Concordance: Will to Power KGW/KSA. The New Nietzsche Studies. Vol. 1:1/2, Fall/Winter 1996, P. 126-153

Singer, Peter "Hegel" (Oxford: Oxford University Press, 1983)

Simmel, Georg "Philosophie der Mode; Die Religion; Kant und Goethe; Schopenhauer und Nietzsche" (Frankfurt am Main: Suhrkamp Verlag, 1995)

Sloterdijk, Peter "Kritik der zynischen Vernunft" (Frankfurt am Main: Suhrkamp Verlag, 1983)

Solomon, Robert C. "Nihilism" in Hondrich, Ted (Ed.) "The Oxford Companion to Philosophy" (Oxford: Oxford University Press, 1995)

Solomon, Robert C. "The Passions: Emotions and the Meaning of Life" (Indianapolis/Cambridge: Hacket Publishing Company, 1993)

Solomon Robert C. & Higgins Kathleen Marie (Ed.) "Reading Nietzsche" (Oxford: Oxford University Press, 1988)

Sorgner, Stefan Lorenz: Heraclitus and Curved Space. In: Universidad Tecnica Particular de Loja (Ed.): Proceedings of the Metaphysics for the Third Millennium Conference (Rom, 5.9.—8.9.2000). Universidad Tecnica Particular de Loja, Loja—Ecuador 2001a: P. 165-170.

Sorgner, Stefan Lorenz "Narzißmus und Nietzsches Wille zur Macht" in Reschke, Renate (Ed.) "Zeitenwende-Wertewende" (Berlin: Akademie Verlag, 2001b), P. 249-254.

Sorgner, Stefan Lorenz "Nietzsche" in Sorgner, Stefan Lorenz & Fuerbeth, Oliver (Ed.) "Musik in der deutschen Philosophie: Eine Einfuehrung" (Stuttgart: Metzler Verlag, 2003), P. 115-134

Sorgner, Stefan Lorenz "Who is the 'music-making Socrates'?" in *Minerva—An Internet Journal of Philosophy* 8 (2004a): 91-113.

Sorgner, Stefan Lorenz: *Vattimo*, "Metaphysik und der Sinn des Lebens." In: *Grenzgebiete der Wissenschaft* 53 (2004b) 2, P. 169-188

Stevens, Anthony "On Jung" (London: Penguin Books, 1990)

Storr, Anthony "Freud" (Oxford: Oxford University Press, 1989)

Turgenev, Ivan "Fathers and Sons" translated from the Russian by Rosemary Edmonds (London: Penguin Books, 1965)

Tzu, Sun "Art of War" (Hertfordshire: Sterling Publishing Company Inc., 1990)

Vattimo, Gianni "Friedrich Nietzsche" translated from the Italian into the German by Klaus Laermann (Stuttgart: Metzler, 1992)

Wilcox, John T. "Truth and Value in Nietzsche: A Study of His Metaethics and Epistemology" (Ann Harbor: University of Michigan Press, 1974)

Wilde, Oscar "The Picture of Dorian Gray" (London: Oxford University Press, 1974)

Wittgenstein, Ludwig "Tractatus Logico-Philosophicus" translated from the German by D. F. Pears & B. F. McGuinness (London: Routledge & Kegan Paul, 1961, 1974)

Wurzer, William S. "Nietzsche und Spinoza" (Meisenheim am Glan: Verlag Anton Hain, 1975)

Index